Church on the ~~Ocean~~

First published in 2006 as a thesis for
the degree of Master of Theology in Missions at
Martin Bucer Theological Seminary
(www.bucer.eu)
and as part of the requirements for the degree of
Master of Theology in Missions
at Whitefield Theological Seminary
(www.whitefield.edu)

Church on the Oceans

A Missionary Vision for the 21st Century

Martin Otto

Copyright © 2007 by Martin Otto
This first edition copyright © 2007 by Piquant Editions Ltd
PO Box 83, Carlisle, CA3 9GR, UK
www.piquanteditions.com

07 08 09 10 11 12 13 14 15 / 6 5 4 3 2 1

ISBN 10: 1-903689-49-X
ISBN 13: 978 1903689 49 3

British Library Cataloguing in Publication Data

Otto, Martin
  Church on the oceans : a missionary vision for the 21st
  century
  1. Merchant mariners - Missions and charities 2. Sailors -
  Religious life 3. Travelers - Religious life 4. Church
  development, New
  I. Title
  266'.00883875

Scripture quotations, unless otherwise stated, are from the Holy
Bible, New International Version, copyright © 1973, 1978, 1984 by
the International Bible Society. Used by permission of Hodder &
Stoughton Publishers, a Member of Hodder Headline Plc Group. All
rights reserved. 'NIV' is a registered trademark of the International
Bible Society. UK trademark number 1448790.

Photographs by Martin Otto
Cover design by Paul Lewis
Cover image of the Berge Stahl used with friendly permission by
Bergesen Worldwide; people inset by Martin Otto

Contents

List of Images

All photographs listed here are copyright by Martin Otto.

Foreword by Patrick Johnstone*

The vision and concepts expressed in this book excite me! That seamen form congregations of worshipping and witnessing Christians is something few people would ever think of. Yet here in this book is the evidence that it is possible. May this vision grow with thousands of such congregations spreading the gospel to other ships and even ports in lands where few other opportunities exist for its proclamation.

A church on a ship? Why not? We have grown so used to the concept that 'church' equals building, while the Bible teaches that church equals people. In English we have the further complication that we commonly use the same word ('church') for the gathering of God's people to praise God and for the building in which they meet. This goes back to the sad deterioration from New Testament Christianity, which was based on people, to a Constantinian Churchianity which was based on structures. Our concept of planting churches is more concerned with places to meet than with disciples to gather. No wonder this church-planting model does not fit the millions of nomadic peoples of the world who live much of their lives in movement – in deserts, steppes, forests and oceans.

Over the last decades of the twentieth century much more effort and thinking was given to how to plant churches among the nomads of this world. We have seen astonishing growth among Roma or Gypsy peoples in Europe and the beginnings of success among such peoples as the nomadic Fulbe of West Africa, the Mongolians on the edge of the Gobi Desert and the Sea Gypsies of Southeast Asia. But what of the millions of seafarers who spend the majority of their working lives away from home and in the difficult transient life on board commercial ships? For too long, ministry among them sought to address their social needs and sometimes focused on evangelism, but to actually plant ship churches was hardly thought of. Yet so many of the major seafaring peoples of the world have many Christians – at least in name – such as the Pacific Islanders, the Filipinos, West Africans and others. Could they not be used of God to reach out to the many Muslim seamen – Arabs, Somalis, Pakistanis, Maldivians, Indonesians?

It is exciting indeed to think of the possibilities of a new generation of seamen's missionaries emerging with a vision to not only evangelize, but also to actually plant churches and link them to a network of shore bases where teaching and teaching materials are to hand as well as to a network of ship churches to connect both seekers and Christians. Is not this vision something for the twenty-first century with all the tools we have – the internet, mobile/cell phones, videos, Bible correspondence courses in print and online and so on?

Many missionaries who have served overseas could find a remarkable new outlet for using their skills and acquired language abilities to enable this vision to be a reality.

May God use this book to envision many and to call some into the challenging ministry of church planting on the oceans.

---

*Patrick Johnstone served for 16 years as a missionary evangelist in Africa before joining the leadership team of WEC International. He is the author of *Operation World* and *The Church Is Bigger Than You Think*. He continues to research and write materials that interpret and enable worldwide church growth in the 21st century.

Foreword by Marco Gmür*

Imagine…a church on a ship!

Close your eyes for a moment and visualize the seven seas. On these waters there are thousands of ships, large and small, all sailing somewhere. Look inside some of these ships and you will discover something you never noticed before.

On some of these ships, seamen meet regularly for worship. There is singing and praise, prayer, preaching, healing, encouraging, collecting of tithes and baptisms. Such meetings are led by elders. And they are more than just meetings. These are the churches of Jesus Christ on the oceans of the world. He is among his people there and is carrying out the will of his Father. He calls and sends out; he glorifies himself through them. And these churches cannot be overcome by Satan. The members of these churches are also members of churches on land, having been sent out for service on the high seas.

It is through these churches that the kingdom of God is growing from day to day!

Isn't this a wonderful vision? While Martin's first book, *Seafarers! A Strategic Missionary Vision*, introduced the concept of outreach to seafarers, this present volume follows on to focus on the need to establish churches on board ships. I invite you to read on and witness this dream becoming reality.

---

*Dr Marco Gmür is a missiologist based in Switzerland. He has an international ministry that reaches out particularly to Muslims.

Acknowledgements

Without the help of some friends, this book would never have been published. I am happy to take this opportunity to thank Dr Allan Adams for the time he dedicated to advising me on this project and also for adding a very important chapter (Chapter 6) to the book. Allan, you were such an encouragement to me throughout the writing of this book. Thank you. Thanks also go to the many port missionaries and seamen who gave me permission to quote their correspondence and reports throughout the book. I also want to thank Mike Wilson, the director of Seamen's Christian Friend Society, who never tired of encouraging and motivating me and thinking things through with me. Thank you also, Mike, for your labours in translating this book into English. My missiologist brother-in-law, Dr Marco Gmür, carefully read the manuscript and challenged me to make it the best book it could be. Marco encouraged me to write this book after finishing *Seafarers! A Strategic Missionary Vision*. Thank you, Marco. Last but not least I must say a big thank you to Patrick Johnstone, for his willingness not only to advise me as to how I should write the book, but also for taking the time to write a foreword. I greatly appreciate, Patrick, that you were never too tired to talk and inspire me on the phone regarding this project. To God be the glory!

Martin Otto
Hamburg, October 2006

1

Finally – A Church for Seafarers!

The body of Christ is vast. It consists of millions of Christians worldwide who love, obey and worship Jesus Christ in thousands and thousands of churches with many different theological backgrounds. But in order to continue to thrive and glorify God, these churches must multiply. And so God equips his people to plant new churches.

Church planting is one of the most thrilling experiences in the world. And, as we see from the New Testament, planting churches is a biblical mandate. There are many books about church planting, and there are many different kinds of churches. There are small churches, house churches, mega churches. Churches are planted in different ways, in different cultures and at different locations. It has perhaps been most difficult to plant churches over the years in those countries where there has been no religious freedom. But believers are mapping out the globe and bringing the gospel to people everywhere – from prisons in Argentina to remote corners of the world, and churches are being planted in these places to the glory of God.

But what about the people we never see? What about people who make their living at sea? These are people you and I do not often think about. These are people who rarely, if ever, have a chance to visit a church on shore. Do those people not have a right to worship Jesus Christ in a church? Are they forgotten by God? Surely not! Christ died as much for seafarers as he died for anyone else. But where is their church?

There are about 1.3 million seafarers who spend between eight and twelve months at sea at a time. Following such a stint they generally spend about two months in their home countries, and then go out again for another eight to twelve months at sea.

They desperately need a living church in which they can worship Jesus Christ.

In the nineteenth century, the Seamen's Friend Society was formed to expand evangelism to this spiritually neglected group of people. They designed a special flag, which was hoisted on the main masthead when there was a church on board. They called it the Bethel flag. The word Bethel means 'house of God' and a Bethel flag indicated 'a ship fitted as a place of worship for sailors.'

God longs to see sailors worship him in his church. To fulfil this mission we need people, churches and mission societies to minister to these forgotten people. Many of the seafarers are from the so-called 10/40 window.[1] Many face all sorts of problems daily, from loneliness and difficulties with their superiors to sickness and communication problems. Because of these issues and the hard lives they lead, many are very open to the gospel.

You can meet with seafarers in international ports on all continents. Ships come to your country, to your ports. Do they hear the gospel there? Who is reaching out to these men? There are still ports in this world without an evangelical witness.

For more than 15 years I have seen that it is possible to have living churches on board ships. Some time ago I visited a huge passenger ship with many different nationalities on board – a thousand seafarers on just one ship – and I was asked to teach their congregation from the word of God during their time in Hamburg while the repairs on the ship were being finished. They met regularly for Bible study, prayer and worship and were eager to share the word of God. On another ship I met with a few believers who told me that they had even chosen elders and that they had communion regularly. This church met several times during the week and they had developed a biblical structure, despite their difficult circumstances. They were a living testimony to the possibility of spiritual life on a ship. They were also a powerful witness to the other sailors on board. In Hamburg we have a small team and cannot visit all 'ship churches' regularly. But even if we cannot visit them all

---

[1] The geographical area between the 10th and 40th degrees latitude, where many unreached countries are located.

we can inform other missionaries in other ports to see to them and nurture them. We can still support them by praying for them and by giving them Bible study correspondence courses, biblical tapes and books, Christian music CDs – all of which encourage their spiritual growth.

Whenever we meet at least two believers we encourage them to start a church on board. Of course such a church is, in many cases, only temporary for the time the sailors are on board. But this should not prevent them from having a living church in which they can glorify God and which will also minister to others on their ship. These sailors have the promises of God in the Bible. One of them that applies particularly to their situation is found in Matthew 18:20: 'Where two or three come together in my name, there am I with them.' Often these very small churches grow in numbers, and as a team we do our best to help and support them.

1. The church on the *Anastasis* represents many different cultures!

Jesus certainly has a big open heart for these men, and he wants them to worship him in a church body. If they have no chance at home to attend church because of their long absences, then they surely must find a way to worship God at sea. If a seafarer spends between 30 and 35 years at sea, he will only be home for about five years in total during that time. Where will he find fellowship and grow in the grace of our Lord Jesus Christ, if not in a church on board? Where will he find comfort and encouragement in times of difficulty, if not in a church on board? Where will he be able to practise his God-given spiritual gifts, if not in a church on board? It is therefore our goal and vision to plant as many ship churches as possible, as well as to nurture those that already exist. As the Holy Spirit establishes these ship churches among different nationalities, they will be a living testimony and a bright shining light to their fellow seafarers and to the glory of God.

2

The Image Problem – What Seamen's Mission Is All About

What do Christians understand when they hear the term 'seamen's mission'? I have been amazed by the kind of misunderstandings I have encountered. First of all, there are many people, and especially in evangelical churches, who have never heard the term 'seamen's mission'. I have had the privilege to talk about seamen's mission in churches and Bible colleges and at mission conferences. Some people think that we sail about the oceans on big ships in order to meet seafarers who have never heard the gospel. Others think that we focus on meeting the social needs of seafarers – so, for instance, if a shipping owner was bankrupt we would take care of the seafarers' practical needs for shelter, food and clothes. Still others imagine that we are a bit like the Salvation Army. One of the problems is that there are many different kinds of missions to seamen, some of which focus on giving practical aid. Christians often run to me with newspaper articles about the fantastic help another seamen's mission is giving to people in one desperate situation or another. Are we not a great bunch of people, they ask, always looking out for more opportunities to help?

While God's word does encourage us to help the poor and needy, and while we cannot show love to people if we are not also willing to help them in practical ways, the needs of the seafarers run far deeper. And so our main motive is to help them spiritually. While social help is very much a part of our work as it supports our spiritual work, our priority is to bring the gospel of Jesus Christ to people on ships, and especially to those who have never heard it.

And so the answer to this question about what we do is a complex one. If our aim is to spread the news of Jesus Christ, do we understand ourselves as an evangelistic organization among seafarers? But we do more than evangelism. Some have said we are responsible for making disciples on ships, not converts. Indeed, we should make disciples because Jesus commanded us to do so (e.g., Matthew 28:19-20). Many worldwide missions have focused on discipleship and have witnessed amazing growth. Even at our own mission conferences we have emphasized the importance of doing discipleship work. Many of our missionaries could give one testimony after another about wonderful times on board ships witnessing seafarers become Christians and then seeing them grow into devoted followers of Jesus. While this is amazing, I'm not satisfied with this definition of seamen's mission.

Christian seamen's missions include many different associations (including, for example, the Seamen's Church Institute and the N.A. Maritime Association). I am personally involved in the Seafarers Mission Hamburg, which is a member of the broader organization called the Seamen's Christian Friend Society. While those of us involved in seamen's mission do share the gospel and make disciples, and while we also want to train more missionaries to do this in the various ports around the world, if we stop there we have an image problem. This definition does not give the full picture of what the seamen's mission is all about. At one of our mission conferences in northern Germany, a large mission agency spoke to us about what God is doing in several parts of the world.

After the meeting I talked with the mission director. 'You're such a big organization with so many missionaries dedicated to reaching the unreached. Would you consider sending some of your missionaries to international ports where nobody is ministering to seafarers?' I asked him. 'This sort of work would fit in well with your goals to share the good news of Jesus with people from the so-called 10/40 window.'

The answer that the director of that very noble mission gave me, in a very convincing voice, was quite a shock. 'You are doing evangelism and discipleship work, but we are doing church planting.'

These words made me think. I was disappointed that this very spiritual man did not recognize ministry to seafarers as an opportunity to reach those in the 10/40 window. I was also disturbed to learn that they did not consider the seamen's mission to be engaged in church planting. I realized that we still had an image problem. Pastors, mission agencies and churches see us as a group of people who evangelize and disciple, but it never occurs to them that we are actually planting churches on ships among seafarers.

This image problem runs so deep that even some missionaries working with seafarers are unclear about the larger vision for this ministry. Some missionaries have been surprised when I have talked with them about church planting on ships and didn't understand what I was trying to say. I am convinced that our difficulties in finding new workers for other ports stem from the fact that we have not clearly defined ourselves as missions that plant churches. That is also why we are often misunderstood.

A port chaplain is someone who meets seafarers who are isolated in the world. When seafarers leave home they also leave their churches. They need more than just a Bible study or a Christian CD. They need a church they can belong to. If they spend some 30 or 35 years at sea, then we must consider the ship or the sea as their home – and they need a church in their home. We all have a church in or near our home. Why should a seafarer not have a church on his ship? If we are not planting churches on ships we are not giving seafarers a chance to have a spiritual home. If we do not plant these churches we are only doing half the job that God has given us.

And to do this work of church planting we need churches, Bible colleges, mission societies and individuals to understand what we are doing and partner with us. There are many seamen's missions worldwide, and many do not preach the gospel but focus mainly on giving practical aid. But there are many of us, in many ports around the world, who share the gospel, do discipleship work – and plant churches. And we would love for the countless students who want to plant churches among people who are neglected, isolated and forgotten to join us. Seamen's ministry offers wonderful opportunities for such work. Our vision is to reach seafarers to bring them to a saving knowledge of our Lord

Jesus Christ and to add them to a living church, to the body of Christ, which can be the very ship they are working and sailing on. These sailing churches will bring glory to God and promote his kingdom wherever they go.

3

New Challenges – New Ideas

Many ships arrive in our ports daily, and often we have no idea who is on board. Will we be able to build relationships with these people, to find the right words and show the love of Christ? Will we have opportunities to share the gospel? Will we meet Christians, Hindus, Muslims, Buddhists or even those who have no religion? It is always a delight to meet dedicated Christian seafarers living their faith on board ship.

Many Christian seafarers are alone on their ship. Some have no-one with whom they can share their problems, sorrows, joys and encouragements. Many do not have the courage to start a Bible study group on their ship. And yet there have been some who have been brave enough to start a Bible study group or prayer meeting in their cabin, or in the crews' or officers' mess room. Some have even felt called by the Lord to minister to their crew mates.

Part of the role of the port chaplain is to encourage our Christian brothers at sea to witness to other seamen and to teach them the word of God. We encourage them to start Bible study groups and/or prayer meetings. When such groups already exist, we make every effort to support them. When we are invited to do so we speak to the sailors and teach them from the word of God while they are in our ports. We pray for, and with, them and we welcome them back when they return to our ports after many months at sea. We have often had the joy of seeing seafarers coming to know the Lord – through on-board Bible studies, through the personal witness of a seafarer, or through evangelistic Bible correspondence courses that many have completed. When time allows we invite seafarers to our homes and churches before we say goodbye again. Many of us write letters to the men at sea and have received some very touching letters back in return. We pray hard for those who are often neglected.

But when their ships set sail, we who remain on shore return again and again to the same questions: Did we do all we could to encourage them in their faith? Were we obedient to do what God wanted us to do for these dear seafarers? Do they have the best materials on board to study the word of God in-depth? Are our colleagues following up with them in the next port? Did we give them all the necessary contact information so that they can find fellowship in the next port? Did we call or write to the next port chaplain to let them know about a Christian fellowship on board a certain ship? Did we try to find churches in the seafarers' various home countries? Whether or not we can answer 'yes' to all of these questions, we commit these seafarers into God's hands as we depend on his grace alone.

Still there is one more vital question we have to ask. If the New Testament speaks so much about churches, why do we port chaplains, and others who are involved in this ministry to seafarers, seldom speak about churches on ships? In her book *An Unconditional Love Story: Meeting the People of the Sea*,[2] Karen Lai says, 'Because modern seafarers spend 80% of their time at sea and only 20% on shore, the Roman Catholic Church has called on its seafaring members to be the Church aboard ship, not merely to wait to be served when arriving in port. Seafarers are called to build community, even a Christian community, among the crew.' At international seamen's mission conferences we have never talked about building or planting churches on ships. We have outlined better follow-up systems and assured each other that we will improve this aspect of our ministries so that the Christians on board will find the fellowship they need. But why have we not discussed planting churches on board for seafarers? Have we unconsciously adopted the old-fashioned (and unbiblical) belief that a church has to have a building of a certain size and an organ? Is a church only a church if it has a certain membership level, five elders and seven deacons?

---

[2] Karen M. Lai, *An Unconditional Love Story: Meeting the People of the Sea* (Beach Park, IL: Mall Publishing, The Maritime Library, 1999).

The New Testament defines 'the church' as people who belong to Jesus and who are called to be in relationship with each other. The word 'church' can refer to all followers of Jesus everywhere, or to a group of believers in a certain location. The New Testament never uses the Greek word translated 'church' to refer to a building or to some place we 'go'. It is not a social organization like the Lions Club or a corporation. Tradition, and especially that stemming from the Roman Catholic Empire (and continuing in Protestantism and evangelicalism), has perverted our understanding of the word such that we say we are 'going to church' when we mean we are going to a building we call 'the church'.

But if we restrict our definition of church to a building, we imply that churches cannot exist on the oceans. Our assumptions restrict us from thinking about the plight of seamen who yearn to belong to a living active church while they are away from their home church. And so we only speak about Bible studies or 'fellowship groups' on ships. The challenge is to think creatively and biblically about what a 'church on a ship' could be.

I have met many seafarers who desperately long for a living church. Some pray regularly for the opportunity to go to church. If the longing is there among seamen, should we not do all we can to meet that need? There can be no church where there is only one believer, but if there are two or three what shall we tell them? We can invite them to our local churches, and surely they will enjoy that fellowship. But during most of their contract they are lonely on the oceans. It is there and then, on the ship, that they need a church. The best way to encourage these believing seafarers would be to equip them to start churches. On-board churches would help them tremendously as they would feel more at home, even though they are far away from their homes and local churches. They would feel a part of God's work. They would have a spiritual home.

When seafarers speak of a church they usually have a tremendous sense of responsibility towards it. They want to be a part of God's church but they also want to see others in God's church. A Bible study group or fellowship group does not generally inspire the same level of dedication and responsibility. For these seafarers church means much more than a fellowship group. One seaman from Syria knew that there were Christians meeting on his ship for Bible study and prayer, but he never attended. One day when his ship was in port, he wanted to leave the ship to find a church in the city. His assumption was that a church could not be on the ship. But when the crew told him that they did already have church on board, he very happily attended.

Most Christians have an incomplete picture of seamen's ministry that begins with evangelism and ends with a bit of discipleship and a vague hope that in their home countries seafarers might find a suitable church. But this misconception does not take the reality of a seafarer's life into account. Often a seafarer who comes to Christ will still have six or nine months left on the ship before he returns home. Where will this tender new believer find church, a body to encourage and teach and nurture him? It is a great sadness that some new converts do not go on with the Lord simply because they have nobody to guide them in their newfound faith, no church on board. Times on shore are few and far between, and even then many seamen are often unable to attend churches on shore for various reasons.

So what does the Bible say that would help us in our mission to plant churches on ships? New Testament churches, from the very beginning, met in different houses – and these houses were called churches. For example, in Romans 16:5 we read, 'Greet also the church that meets at their house.' Colossians 4:15 says, 'Give my greetings to the brothers at Laodicea, and to Nympha and the church in her house.' In 1 Corinthians 16:19 we find the following greeting: 'Aquila and Priscilla greet you warmly in the Lord, and so does the church that meets at their house.' In Paul's letter to Philemon (verse 2) he sends greetings to the church that met in his home. Acts 2:46 tells us that the believers meeting in these small house churches even took the bread and wine to remember the Lord: 'They broke bread in their homes and ate together with glad and sincere hearts.' It is clear, then, that it was and is valid for the church to exist in places like the living room of a house or a mess room on a ship. The house (ship) church movement has a vision to plant churches everywhere for the purpose of fulfilling the Great Commission through evangelism, discipleship and world mission. The house (ship) church can be an effective way to reach out to all nations.

As we have seen, Christians need to take seriously Jesus' promise in Matthew 18:20: 'where two or three come together in my name, there am I with them.' This is literally the smallest possible church, but we should not neglect it because it is small. The important thing is that Christ, with his promises, presence and power, is in their midst. The Holy Spirit himself dwells there. Is that not enough to start a church?

And when the Holy Spirit is present this very small church will grow – spiritually and also in number. Nobody would say that a church consisting of two or three seamen is perfect – we always expect growth from the Lord. But to not accept this kind of church as legitimate would be to deny seafarers their right to worship God and grow together in the body of Christ. Nowhere does the Bible assign a number that qualifies a group to be called church. God wants his people to worship him, and this is possible even if there are only two or three.

Many mature Christians from different denominations around the world are convinced that the most effective form of church is to meet in a house, and many of these people belong to a large movement called the house church movement. House churches are particularly strong in times of trouble, persecution and suffering in places where religious freedom does not exist. On ships with difficult or extreme officers, a church that meets in the cabin of a seaman could fulfil a real need. Seafarers would benefit tremendously from this kind of church. They would be able to pray and worship God at all times.

> Like today, the Church in Acts was not a building, but a community of people, with real needs and real struggles. Because of the fierce anti-Christian sentiment rampant in the first century, church members huddled together in homes and secret meetings, often the only times of relative safety they enjoyed. Despite these constricting circumstances, the Church worshiped, broke bread, learned and taught, and raised up leaders. Never since has the Church been as united in purpose and spirit. (Acts 1:12 – 2:3; 2:42–47; 4:32–37; 5:1–11; 6:1–6). The church is starting to see itself completely differently – that is one trend which is

growing stronger. It is no longer understood as a single organized fellowship (with a pastor, a building, a programme and a more or less creative name), but as an organic community of Christians in towns and regions, the sum of the members of related house churches, cells, groups and fellowships. This gives the church, as in the times of Acts, a regional instead of denominational identity.[3]

I do believe that we will see a ship church movement in the future. Christians around the world need to embrace the truth that a ship church is of God. It might be a temporary church, maybe lasting only for one contract of nine months. It will not always be easy to plant a church on board, but the fact that there are still no churches on board the majority of ships should not discourage us from establishing churches. The ship churches that do already exist are loved and cared for by our Lord Jesus. Christians on shore need to support such churches through their prayers and, if possible, in practical ways as well. Churches located in harbour areas can reach out to seafarers in their port, befriending them and sharing their vision of church on the oceans.

---

[3] From the missions catalyst dated 13 Oct., 2004 at www.calebproject.org.

4

What History Reveals about Churches for Seafarers on Ships and on Shore

Most ships do not have a church on board. There is still a lot to do to make seafarers aware that they can be in a church even though they are far away from their home church and sailing on the oceans. My colleagues and I always invite seafarers we meet to churches in Hamburg, and they always seem to enjoy it. Seafarers often long to see a church after sailing on the oceans for a long time. Some really do consider a visit to church as one of their highlights of their sea contract. When Christian seafarers come with us to churches in Hamburg, they often share their testimonies and some are even courageous enough to sing songs for us. They enjoy and are tremendously encouraged by the fellowship with other Christians. They continue their journeys with new joy.

One of the most thrilling books on the subject of churches for seafarers is *Seamen's Missions: Their Origin and Early Growth* by Dr. Roald Kverndal.[4] In this wonderful book we find not only the history of seamen's missions, but also many stories of churches that were founded by pastors on shore for seafarers who came to various ports around the world. Christians in the nineteenth century realized how much seafarers were in need of a living church. Seafarers' living conditions were very difficult and, because of the many problems they were facing, they were open to God's word – perhaps even more so than they are today. These early churches had two purposes. First, they preached Christ to

---

[4] Roald Kverndal, *Seamen's Missions: Their Origin and Early Growth* (Pasadena, CA: William Carey Library, 1986).

those seafarers who had not yet accepted Christ and, second, they sought to teach those who were Christians so that they could find fellowship and grow in their faith.

> It seems only fitting that a church maritime should first have manifested himself at sea. Sources are scant. However it is safe to assume, that those pioneer missionaries who, during the earliest era of the church, put to sea in order to spread the faith beyond their own borders used the opportunity while on shipboard to share the Gospel with sailors and fellow passengers alike. It comes as no surprise that ways were sought to safeguard the spiritual life of those who spent much of their life at sea. Thus, it was required that provision be made for mariners to observe days of fasting and abstinence while in service. Also it became a common custom for ships to carry with them to sea some sacred object, crucifix, image, picture or other form of church symbol. This could be connected to the mast. In this case the foot of the mast would become a common place of prayer, and William Tyndale, the English reformer, informs us that, 'shipmen in peril of death, if a priest be not by, shrive themself unto the mast'. In some cases a ship could carry an altar, even a small chapel.[5]

We also read about the Reverend W.H. Angas,

> who distributed large quantities of Scriptures and tracts in English, German and other languages. He also published in German a book called *Good News on the Sea* which was greatly circulated and excited considerable 'concern for sailors'. He founded a Sunday school primarily for seamen's children which eventually grew to great proportions and, incidentally, stimulated the institution of Sunday Schools elsewhere in Germany. He even obtained the sanction of the City Senate for the establishment of a floating chapel for Hamburg. A floating chapel remained only a desideratum, for want of funds, however, some form of alternative did become available when a new English Reformed Church was opened in July 1826 not far from the shore. Here a 200-seat Seamen's Gallery was incorporated.

---

[5] Kverndal, *Seamen's Missions*, pp. 5–6.

...in order to succeed in shaking Satan's empire on the sea, Angas was convinced that preaching and circulating Scripture and tracts, however basic, was not enough. Wherever he could, he sought to supplement this by promoting Sunday Schools for seamen's children, Bible classes for adult seamen, and depots for marine libraries. Always, he proved particularly alert to the needs of foreign seamen, eagerly embracing opportunities to minister to them in German, Dutch and French. When working in Liverpool in 1828 he published brief hymnals in German and Dutch for his Floating Chapel services with seamen from those countries.[6]

Christians in this era had great passion to start churches for seafarers.

In *The Sailors Magazine* of the American Seamen's Friend Society there was a frequent topic of discussion of a 'Seamen's Communion' or a 'Christian Church' organized specifically for seamen. ... Why should Christian seamen be left spiritually 'homeless' bereft of both the sacrament of holy communion, and that 'bond of brotherly love' which could be acquired by belonging to a church made up of seafaring fellow believers? Some suggested organizing an international Christian fellowship of seafarers. However, the situation was evidently not ripe for a structure of worldwide dimensions. Instead there emerged a form of localized communion, based on individual mariners' churches. Admission would generally be open to seafarers and residents who (1) gave 'satisfactory evidence of a change of heart', and (2) agreed to a confession of faith and form of covenant of broadly evangelical and nonsectarian content. Boston began in 1830. Afterwards a parallel pattern of church organization was adopted by mariners' churches elsewhere, for example in Philadelphia (later in 1830), Baltimore (1837), and Portland, Maine (1840). Abroad the same model was followed, for example in Le Havre (1832) and Honolulu (1837).[7]

---

[6] Kverndal, *Seamen's Missions,* pp. 256, 258.
[7] Kverndal, *Seamen's Missions,* p. 488.

In the little brochure called 'People that I Met' (Menschen die ich erlebte) from the Deutsche Seemannsmission in Bremerhaven, we read the words of a German pastor, Mr Wilhelm Schneider, who had a church on shore for seafarers in Bremerhaven in the early 1950s. 'Sailors loved to attend church there. They had regular church services every Sunday … in the church for the seafarers on shore they not only had seafarers as church members, but also their wives and mothers who were faithful attendees. These mothers, wives and friends were a church that made the seafarer welcome when he arrived with his ship in port. The older women in church were the praying force with a special task of the Lord to pray for the sailors.'[8]

A very well-known man of God, Dawson Trotman, the founder of the Navigators in the United States, began his ministry by sharing God's love with seafarers. He would invite seafarers to local churches on shore and his vision was to train seafarers so that they would become missionaries on their ships. They held Bible studies on board ships and also on shore, yet there is no evidence that Dawson himself, or the seafarers he trained, started any churches on board these ships.[9]

There are many more examples of churches for seamen on shore and also floating churches, especially in the United States. Floating churches were ships dedicated for the purpose and were permanently moored or anchored. Very little, however, is known about churches that were active on board ships sailing on the oceans. Part of the reason for this may be that seafarers were afraid to call their fellowships on board 'churches' for fear of being labelled heretics.

---

[8] 'Menschen die ich erlebte' (Bremerhaven: Deutsche Seemannsmission an der Unterweser in Bremerhaven, Ditzen & Co., 1955), p. 12.
[9] Betty Skinner, *Daws: A Man Who Trusted God* (Colorado Springs, CO: Navpress, 1993).

5

Existing Churches on Ships

The concept of churches on ships is not a new one. In fact, there have been churches in various forms on ships for many years. Unfortunately we do not hear all the testimonies of churches on ships because some ships never come to our ports. The following is a report from *Challenge*, a Christian newspaper in England.

Luxury liner *Queen Elizabeth 2* hit the headlines, when disgruntled passengers complained about a refit not being completed in time. What the pampered passengers did not realize was that things might have been much worse if there had not been a group of mainly Filipino crew members praying for the ship and her passengers.

Fernando and Bert lead a group of about 25 Christians in regular praise and worship meetings in the crew's library. Whenever the *QE2* berths at Southampton David Thomson, port chaplain of the Seamen's Christian Friend Society, is on board to encourage and help them. There is seldom an opportunity for the crew to visit his home, because the few hours the *QE2* is in port are taken up with passengers' luggage and other duties. 'It was tragic when a few years ago the *QE2* struck rocks and had to go to Hamburg for repairs,' says David, yet God used the free time the crew had. 'The port missionary in Hamburg, Martin Otto, held several group Bible Studies, explaining who Christ is and the need to take him into our lives as our personal Lord and Saviour.

'I consequently saw the result of this when the ship came back to Southampton. Nine men spoke of how since they put Christ in first place of their lives many aspects of their lives were changing. They spoke of beginning to see practical help in the Bible.'

One of the young men, Eddie, who was then with the liner, became like a pastor to these young Christians and helped them to establish the 'church' which is now flourishing aboard the *QE2*. For many years now the church on *QE2* has been a tremendous blessing for many seamen. I had the joy to be invited to teach the word of God and I was amazed to see how well this church was established. The Seamen's Christian Friend Society's network of 'Port Links' around the world is a lifeline to the isolated Christian seafarer. These 'links' are often ordinary families living in the port area. A phone call to the family results in an invitation to come to their home and share a meal and the sailor does not have to join his ship mates wandering aimlessly through the town and being exposed to all sorts of temptations.

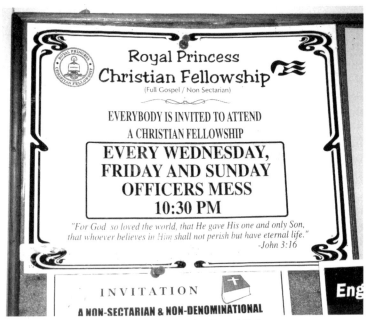

2. Invitation for a church meeting on the *Royal Princess*

The *Royal Princess*, a large luxury liner, came to Hamburg several times. On board I met many Filipino seafarers but also crew members from Mexico, India, Portugal, Canada, England and Nepal. I was always amazed to see how many people on board showed an interest in spiritual matters. When I boarded the ship last in September 2003 I took a huge bag full of tracts, Bible study courses, Bibles, inspirational books and Christian music (worship CDs). While I was sitting in the crew's mess room I met Bernie, the pastor of the ship's church. Both Bernie and I were amazed that, after a short time, all the Christian material that I offered to the crew was gone. People were longing for more of God and were happy to buy a Christian music CD or a *Jesus* film. They were also delighted to receive the tracts, Bibles and Bible study courses we provided for them. When I preached, people listened very carefully. I think they were so interested in spiritual matters because a Christian church had existed on this cruise liner for quite a long time. Some of the Christians told me that the church on *Royal Princess* meets at least three times a week, a gathering of between ten and fifteen Christians.

On Wednesdays they have a prayer meeting from 10:30 p.m. until 12 a.m. On Fridays they meet for Bible study from 10:30 p.m. until 12 a.m. On Sundays their worship service begins at 10:30 p.m. and sometimes lasts until 1:30 a.m. During this service they listen to testimonies from various crew members, sing, pray and also hear preaching – from a tape or from a fellow crew member. Their numbers peaked at about 30 a few years ago. Since then many of the Christians had gone on vacation[10] or moved to work on other ships. Some Christians on board cannot attend the church because they have to work during the meetings.

'How does the church grow?' I asked the pastor.

Bernie answered, 'First, we try to make sure that everybody is having a regular quiet time. Also, we meditate upon the word of God together. Third, we encourage members to share their faith with those they meet and also to share testimonies during our worship service. Fourth, we train people to start preaching or at least to share something from the Bible. And, lastly, we all listen to preaching tapes.'

Bernie also told me that in recent years quite a number of seafarers have come to know Christ because of the evangelistic efforts of those involved in the church. They had elected two

---

[10] Seafarers go on vacation for two to three months until they join their next ship.

elders whose responsibility it was to lead the church. Every first Sunday of the month the church on board the *Royal Princess* breaks bread. They also take regular offerings, which they have used in the past to buy musical instruments and to support a missionary work in Chile. Bernie also told me that, each time an elder goes home on vacation, the church gives him US$100 for his local home church in the Philippines, to help build the church there.

'And what do the elders do when they go back to their home church?' I asked Bernie. 'What would their position there be?'

'The elders go home as members of their local church,' Bernie explained, 'submitting to the eldership and leadership of their home church in the Philippines.'

It is clear from the example of the *Royal Princess* and others that, once a church is established on board, it has a positive influence on everyone. Christians involved in the church grow in their faith and develop loving and caring relationships with one another. Church members also pray for their mates and find they are much more willing to listen to the gospel if there is a church on board. A church can create a positive atmosphere that even non-Christians notice and appreciate.

* * *

The World is another ship with a church on board that I have been able to visit. *The World* is unique in that it has many apartments. These are sold to people who can afford them, and people live on the ship as long as they like. It was a miracle that the ship's security officers allowed Ecki Breitenmoser, a Bible college student (and now a full-time port missionary in Bremerhaven) and myself to board *The World*. When we came to the gangway and asked for permission, the crew manager answered: 'People who bring the word of God are always welcome.'

Our hosts even led us to the crew's mess room, where we met with the Filipino seafarers. At lunchtime many came to see what we had to offer. As on the *Royal Princess,* we were amazed that in a matter of half an hour we had exhausted our supply of Bibles, tracts, Bible courses, worship CDs and *Jesus* films. They bought everything! Ecki went back to the car to get more literature – and 30 minutes later the big literature bag was empty again. And still the seafarers were asking for more. So we left the ship and drove to the nearest Christian bookstore for some more material, which we offered them at their afternoon coffee break.

The Christians on board had just started a church, and this hunger for the word of God among the seafarers encouraged them greatly. Because they saw who wanted the Bibles, Bible study courses, *Jesus* films and Christian music, they knew who was interested in spiritual matters. They knew who to pray for, follow up with and invite to their church meetings. When the church leader witnessed the tremendous hunger in these men, tears rolled down his face. He never imagined that so many people on his ship would want so much Christian material. The church had begun with about a dozen people who regularly attended, and after this experience they were very optimistic that this number would soon grow.

* * *

The most exciting ship I've visited in the last 16 years in the port of Hamburg is a luxury yacht belonging to a wealthy Saudi Arabian. People say that the owner is one of the advisers to the king. While the owner only visits his yacht every so often, when he does he arrives in his own plane. He is transported from the airport in a huge Mercedes, escorted by his bodyguards. It is actually sort of a secret ship – nobody is allowed to visit, and the crew is nervous when he is there. The ship carries neither cargo nor passengers but is essentially a showpiece of the 'big man' from Saudi Arabia.

I did not, of course, know any of this when I approached the gangway to try to visit the yacht. The security officer who met me asked who I was and told me plainly that nobody was allowed to visit. So I left, and our church prayed for God to give us an opportunity to visit this ship. Shortly after this time of prayer I made one more attempt to visit the ship. A young second officer, who later told me that he was a born-again Christian too, met me and allowed me to enter.

In the mess room I met with about 20 Filipino seafarers who were delighted to see somebody from the seamen's mission. Several people were eager to have Bibles in their own language, which is Tagalog. As the ship stayed several weeks in dry dock,

I had time to develop friendships with crew members. The captain of the yacht was not happy when I asked him whether I was allowed to hold Bible studies on board. He said that nobody would be interested and that the ship belonged to a Muslim. He did, however, allow me to meet with the seafarers in a nearby container. I met with the crew for Bible study, invited them to our home and also conducted personal Bible studies with individuals. Our time together was very encouraging, and before they sailed two men gave their lives to Christ.

Three years later, the ship came back to Hamburg for some repairs. I boarded the ship and found that many of the crew still there. There was also a very dedicated Christian Filpina seawoman, who invited everybody for church meetings on board. And so, there and then, a church was started. They worshipped God, had Bible studies and prayed together. There were between eight and ten crew members involved in this church (out of a Filipino crew of 20), and they were eager to tell the other crew members about Jesus Christ. They invited me to speak at their ship-church about prayer and I enjoyed the wonderful fellowship with these brothers and sisters immensely.

* * *

It is always good to hear that a church on board a ship has gained official recognition. Following is an email message I received from a female information technology (IT) officer:

> Hello brother Martin, how are you? I'm very pleased to inform you that we are growing in numbers! Not only Filipinos, we have Indian and South African members. Sadly, that was my last Bible study this contract, as I'm leaving for vacation on Saturday. But I'm glad to know that I'm leaving a great team … and I know that the Lord is with this church that he will bless them with more workers and speakers. Brother Melchor is on day shift next month so he can be with them during fellowships. We were able to purchase a guitar – we have new members who have gifts in music. That's really exciting! Also, we already have on-board management's approval/permit for the Boudicca[11] church – so

---

[11] The ship's name is *Boudicca*. Many call their church after their ship's name.

we can gather at the crew day room officially, distribute flyers and post invitations at the crew area. We really thank the Lord for all the blessings that he's giving us.

My co-worker, Volker Lamaack, told me about another very small but yet lively church. On the *Sierra Express*, a container ship that regularly runs the route between Hamburg and Central America, he met with three people from the Philippines and one man from Bulgaria. Here is how Volker experienced church on that particular ship:

> I had been visiting this ship for ten years. Every six weeks they were in Hamburg. Many seafarers on the ship studied Bible courses. One of them, a Filipino called Sebastian Florante, was saved several years ago and sailed again and again on the same ship. The last time I was in contact with him he was studying his nineteenth Bible course! Another crew member was Georgi Dimitrov from Bulgaria. He was also a devoted follower of Christ. In April he asked me if we could have communion on the ship's church. This was a new thing for me. Over the past 11 years nobody had ever asked me to have communion on board. Two hours later we sat together with bread and wine and worshipped the Lord Jesus in our communion service. It was a very moving time together. Sebastian, Georgi and Jerald, who is also a Christian, met regularly every week for Bible study and prayer. They practised the four basic elements of the church found in Acts 2:42 – fellowship, prayer, teaching and the breaking of bread and wine. After Georgi went on vacation we received the very sad news that he had died in a car accident. Shortly after Georgi's death the other two fellows finished their contracts and went home on vacation. So I guess that was the end of that small but living church on board a container vessel.

While some ship churches, like this one, may exist for only a year, others continue for many years – such as those on board the *Queen Elizabeth 2* and the *Royal Princess*. But this uncertainty about a church's future or longevity should never stop people from planting churches on these ships. Seafarers need churches just as we do, and God can bring many blessings and much growth in even a relatively short space of time.

Volker and I met with another church on the *Saga Rose*, a beautiful old passenger ship that was in dry dock in Hamburg for some repairs. When we boarded the ship we immediately came into contact with several believers who enthusiastically told us about their captain, who was also their pastor for their ship's church. The captain was away on holiday at the time, but it was obvious that he was a good Christian witness to the crew and officers. He organized the church meetings on a Sunday, and they enjoyed some wonderful times worshipping God. The captain taught the Bible to those who attended the church and they learned not only to keep the faith for themselves but also to share Jesus with others. The church grew in number and when I was invited to preach there one Sunday there were about 15 people attending.

* * *

Most of the work we are engaged in through the seamen's mission focuses on commercial and cruise ships, but we also have an outreach to military ships. Following is an email from Thomas K. Hayden, on board the *USS Nicholas*:

> On the second day underway one of my ship mates asked about getting involved in church services and sought help with his decision to 'turn over a new leaf'. By the third day underway I have had three people inquire about a Bible. On day four Jason informed me that one of our ship mates would be joining the service and bringing his guitar. The 'excitement' of what goes on with our group is spreading and I look forward to each day just to see who God is going to send my way. It has now been six days at sea and two more people have asked for Bibles. I am preparing my first Sunday service for the deployment and need your prayers. Week one is over and another ship mate asked about receiving a Bible. I am almost out of Bibles! I sent an email regarding the lack of Bibles to David and Nancy in North Carolina, who passed my request to their friend in the Gideon's. One of our upcoming ports is near a facility that should have Bibles I can pick up. If those options fail, I will let you know. I left my wife, Cindy, and daughters, Kayla and Kelsey, in Portsmouth, VA. ... I have a copy of the Naval Christian Fellowship (NCF) Hospitality List,[12]

but I don't see anyone for the areas we are going to. With regard to my Bible dilemma, I am anxiously awaiting an answer from my friends in North Carolina. I have the possibility of picking up Bibles from an upcoming port. Today was my second Sunday at sea with an amazing attendance of 18 sailors this afternoon during Sunday service. We were able to pass out some Bibles and add some people to the list for the daily devotion that I send out. Each Sunday I am taking up a prayer list at the service to forward to praying friends. Sailors face a myriad of problems once we set sail from home and it is my sincere hope and desire to help them through these problems by guiding them towards the strength of God. Currently the space I teach in holds 24 people. When we grow beyond that number, I will have to move to the mess decks which hold 40-plus people. I wish you could see my excitement! My ship was visited by the admiral in charge of our entire battle group. He gave us a nice speech then opened the floor to questions, specifically asking if he could do anything for us. So, I raised my hand and simply stated, 'I need Bibles.' He asked what kind. I said, 'pocket size and regular, NIV and KJV'. He then asked me how many I needed and I said, 'As many as you are willing.' At that, he called in his aide and said, 'Get Chief Hayden some Bibles. Get big ones, small ones and a lot of them!' (Before I continue, let me give you a little background information. I am on my ship in the middle of the ocean. His ship is a long way off, somewhere else in the ocean.) By the time his helicopter came to pick him up a few hours later, he delivered six boxes to me containing over two hundred new Bibles. There are hard-backed, paper-backed, small Bibles, NIV and KJV. Let us praise our Lord, for he is true to his Word...'ask and you shall receive'. I thank everyone else for their offer to send Bibles, but now I am glad to say I no longer have room for anymore! Each day I stop by the place where I keep the Bibles and notice a few more have been taken!

On 29 May 2006 I received another email from Thomas:

First of all, I would like to thank you for the encouraging emails

---

[12] This hospitality list is given to all NCF serving members to enable them to find Christian fellowship wherever they go in the world.

that you continue to send. I am a person that loves the company of family and friends and although my band of brothers is growing out here it is still very comforting to receive correspondence from you. It doesn't surprise me to tell you that we have not only reached, but superseded, the capacity of the room we use for worship services. So it was with great pleasure that I announced today that our group would be moving to the mess decks because it holds over 40 people instead of only 24 people. In fact, we may even be adding another guitar player to our service which will bring us up to three guitars, one bongo and a keyboard. Your prayers are certainly helping with the momentum of God's work on this ship!!! I wish I had the words to describe to you the level of enthusiasm for our Lord. Jesus is becoming a hot topic on board the *USS Nicholas*.

And the following update arrived from Thomas on 11 June 2006:

The only way for the word of God to spread at sea is via the lay readers.[13] Personally I have found this to be a highly neglected duty on each of my ships upon arrival. It is nothing less than a burning desire for me to get sailors excited about Christ. On my first ship, *USS Robert G. Bradley*, I started a weekly Bible study and led Sunday service underway. On my first deployment it was a huge challenge because although I was excited to do this, I had no formal or even informal training.

During my second deployment I had the advantage of lessons learned and some navy training from the chaplains on base. My wife bought me a keyboard so I could add some music to the program and I was blessed with a ship mate who could lead us in singing.

By the time I started my third deployment I had a solid system down and a well-established group of believers and a regular

---

[13] Sailors that hold the title of 'lay reader' are hand picked by their commanding officer, recommended by their home church, and sent to a school to train them for the job. On ships that do not have a large enough crew to employ a chaplain, lay readers are the only means of getting the word of God to the sailors. They are not allowed to preach, only to teach.

attendance of 21 sailors. While I was on shore duty I spent a great deal of time thinking of what I could do to make my next ship a fertile field for reaping a huge harvest for the Lord. To my surprise, when I arrived on the *USS Nicholas,* there was already a lay reader on board. So I didn't try to assume that position. Within about a month I was personally asked by the captain to serve as the lay leader. The awesome thing about that is that I had not mentioned anything about my desires to fill that position.

I am convinced that God, who knows all, wanted me to get started with my plans for this ship. The one thing I learned from my last ship was that singing and music are vital to the service. It sets the stage for true worship and brings an aura of togetherness. I cannot lead the music by myself, so I immediately began a search for someone who was willing to do so. Thankfully, about three weeks before my first deployment on this ship, STG2 Jason Cash was transferred here at the last minute because we had a sudden loss of the personnel that can do his job. He is the son of a Christian music singer and has a natural talent for playing the guitar and singing. To my great surprise he immediately volunteered to help. As a result, the entire deployment was a complete success. We established a wonderful fellowship and even created the Nicholas Praise Team. Jason and I have spent the last nine months praying and preparing for this deployment.

In January I started a daily devotion email distribution list. These emails included a morning and evening devotion and a list of Bible chapters to read each day in order to read the Bible in one year. At first I had about 15 people sign up and now I am up to 45 people. My church at home has given me student guides and instructor lesson plans to teach Sunday service throughout the deployment. This has been well accepted by everyone who attends.

I also have an on-going prayer list that gets filled out every Sunday and disseminated via the distribution list. Our service usually runs anywhere from an hour to 1½ hours. We have grown from about 16 people regularly attending to over 24 people. In fact, last Sunday we had almost 30 in attendance. The excitement of the group that I fellowship with seems to multiply each day. I don't have to walk far one way or the other on this ship without running into a brother in Christ. We are in a constant state of uplifting one another and praising our Savior. It is so awesome to see God work his way through this crew.

Jason changed our name from 'Protestant Lay Services' to N. P. C. (Nicholas Protestant Church). Everyone really liked that, I think. This is a wonderful blessing that I am truly honored to be a part of. I look forward with great anticipation each day as to what our Lord will do. We are called to tell others about Christ around the world. What better way than about a ship with a captive audience?

3. **USS Nicholas** – a church meeting at the end of a hard day working on this navy ship

Nathan Senior works on a British navy ship, and he sent me the following communication:

The 'church' on board *HMS Liverpool* has been a slow labour of love for three and half years … the Alpha course has been a great tool in reaching many of our ship's company. Please allow me to give you a brief history … I joined *HMS Liverpool* towards the end of 2002. When I joined her I found that I already knew quite a few of the crew members, which made my life easier … to the best of my knowledge I was the only confessing Christian on board at the time. *HMS Liverpool*'s church … I must be honest with you, Martin. I had never considered our little group of believers as a church until you emailed me and our intention was never to set up a church as such … all we wanted to do was tell our ship mates that Jesus loves them and that our great Father wants to adopt them. Well, as I have already said, I have been on *HMS Liverpool* for some time now and although since day one I have told my mess mates and ship mates about Jesus, none of them wanted to confess him as saviour. Last year, before we sailed for the Caribbean, there were just two confessing Christians on board – myself and my dear brother Alan Murrel. We shared the gospel with our ship mates and fellowshipped when we got the chance. I'll be honest with you – for a long time I had been having some serious doubts about my effectiveness as a Christian. I was ready to leave the Navy altogether. I kept on asking God why I had been on board for so long and seen no results from my witness … not even a moral change in my friends. But the Lord said to keep on working, so I did. Before we left England for the Caribbean another Christian joined the crew. Her name is Elspeth Isbister, and she was the medical officer for that particular deployment. At the time she was unaware of any Christians on board and had been asking God for help as she was also struggling with being a Christian at sea. So we fellowshipped and prayed together. … Now one of the wonderful things about the Royal Navy is that it is governed by a law called the Articles of War, of which article one insists on the rightful divine worship of Almighty God every Sunday! Up until this point I had been taking church services when we had no chaplain embarked … but now we had Elspeth … She was a great asset to the church effort as she plays guitar! This made the hymn singing easier and more fun … At this point maybe I should say that on Sundays at sea we get about 25 – 35 or more coming to the church services. A mixture of officers and ratings.[14] I'll be honest – most of them come along because the chefs put on some good after-church cakes. At the half-way point of the deployment we had a stand-off period in Barbados.

---

[14] Ratings are all seafarers working on the deck, engine or kitchen who do not have the rank of officer.

It was whilst we were here that God started his mission to *HMS Liverpool* ... one night when I was in one of the clubs with my friends, one of the lads called Ashley Steinschauer came up to me and started telling me how bad his life was and how he wanted it to change. I asked him to leave the club with me. We went outside and down the road a bit to a church and sat down on the doorstep. Now over the door of this church was a Bible verse. (I can't tell you what the verse was.) I started to tell Ash the gospel from that verse. A few days later Ash told me that he had asked Jesus into his life! Well I was near tripping when he told me this. While all this had been going on with me Elspeth had been running a campaign to tell the officers on board about Jesus. Two of the guys from the wardroom were really interested and had also engaged me in conversation about the Lord. First up was a guy called Jeeves Tour ... he's an Indian by descent. He was born into a Hindu family, but he had married a Christian. He had been going to church with his wife and did believe the Bible but was struggling to commit himself to it. After some gentle teaching and a visit to a church in Barbados called the People's Cathedral, where the minister gave an alter call at the end, Jeeves was the first man standing and walking to the front! Matt Hulse was the name of the other guy. Both he and Elspeth had been through a bit of a trial together, and Matt wanted to know how she had been able to remain so peaceful about the whole episode. She told him that God had given her peace and grace to deal with the problem. He had been asking her more and more about Jesus and again it was at the People's Cathedral that he asked Jesus into his life! All three are now on other ships in the fleet serving God and telling others about him! Now back to the *HMS Liverpool* ... now that the number of Christians had grown we were very keen to meet for prayer and Bible study at every occasion ... we came up with the idea of 'espresso prayer'. Not everybody has the time to have a whole hour of dedicated Bible and prayer time, but everybody generally is up early, so we try and meet up most mornings for a coffee and prayer. It's good because it's focused and intense, just like an espresso. However, we were all keen to keep up our work of witness to the ship. What we needed as well as our own personal witness was a concerted organized effort to reach out to the ship. After the deployment we got back home and over summer leave we all prayed and asked the Lord for direction in this matter. Through various meetings and conversations and things I like to call 'God incidences' (no such thing as coincidences), the Alpha for Forces course became the obvious tool for the outreach programme. The Alpha has been a great tool and vehicle for the gospel, and during this current deployment (to the Falkland Islands) our great and glorious Father has used it and us (how humbling) to bring about ten people to own him as Lord and Saviour, and another 60-plus people were actually considering matters of faith and eternity! *God is good!* Our church on *HMS Liverpool,* as every church, has been built because the Lord built it with us! None of us are super Christians, but we have a super Father who loves us and loves seafarers … John 3:16 … For God so loved seafarers that he gave his one and only Son that all seafarers who believe in him shall not run aground, be lost at sea or drown but have eternal life in heaven's glorious port!

Here is what Captain David Warden-Owen of the *Saga Rose* said about his church on board.

Dear Martin,

I am only too pleased to assist you with your survey of churches aboard ships. I believe that Christian Masters have a unique ministry and I realise that I'm privileged to be in a position of influence to spread the Good News to both passengers and crew. Traditionally on British cruise ships the master normally led the church service on sea days. I say normally because I have occasionally met one or two who will not do so. Ever since I became captain in 1990 I have always encouraged my crew to meet for Christian fellowship and Bible study and, whenever time permits, I will attend. Here on the *Saga Rose*, we are blessed to have a good many 'born-again, Spirit filled' believers amongst the crew. As you know, the Filipino crew love to sing and the praise and worship time at the fellowship meeting is so anointed that outsiders cannot fail to feel the presence of the Holy Spirit. The same applies when they sing as the ship's choir to open the passenger Sunday worship service in the grand ballroom. Some 400 of the 550 passengers will, on average, attend and be visibly moved by the presence of the Holy Spirit. Some possibly experience this here for the very first time in their adult lives. So it is a very privileged and unique opportunity to be used for the kingdom in this way. To digress a little … I joined *Saga Rose* in 1997, having served on Cunard Line ships, including the *QE2*, for 24 years and was poised to take command of that fine ship. However, God had another plan for my life and as doors began to close in Cunard due to my belief, another door opened in *Saga Rose*. My walk with God continued unhindered initially, and the Christian ethos on the *Saga Rose* became a hallmark of the passenger cruise experience. So much so that requests were made for passenger Christian fellowship and Bible study. We prayed about it, and God answered our prayer by sending us Brian and Angela Mills, a lovely couple who were to be the professional dance team on the 2000 World Cruise. Apart from being a tremendous asset to the ship, they are spirit-filled Christians who would start up the passenger Bible study on board. This has now become a regular feature of the cruise and, when they are not on board, I facilitate the gathering. On some cruises as many as 50 of the passengers will attend. But the enemy is at work and comes in many guises to hinder God's work aboard this fine and elegant lady of the sea. We know that we will experience persecution, but we stand on the promise of Psalm 133 that, being united in Christ, we will receive God's blessing. Thank you for allowing me to share our ministry here on the *Saga Rose* and I too hope to meet you one of these days. May God bless your work abundantly.

Captain David Warden-Owen

In the early years of our ministry we met with many seafarers from Ghana, Nigeria, Cameroon and Ethiopia. Unfortunately, not many seafarers from these countries come to our port these days due to economic problems. However, on these ships we were able to witness God's living church on the oceans. Especially on ships from Ghana, Nigeria and Ethiopia we saw a desire to live in a worshiping community and to glorify God in church on board. There were several established churches on board ships from the Nigerian National Shipping Lines. The Nigerians in particular placed a high value on having a pastor. I still remember some of the ships where the crew met two or three times a week to worship God in their cabins. The number of seafarers who attended these meetings was usually quite high – sometimes half of the crew or more.

There are surely more ship churches floating across the oceans, and yet the Christian world does not recognize them because they do not hear from them and they do not see them. Sometimes it seems as if this is a forgotten church. Yet God sees them and nurtures them. God has a deep love for them and Christ gave himself for his church on the oceans, too.

6

Living Church on the OM Ships

Our family lived on board the Operation Mobilisation ships *MV Logos* and *MV Doulos* for 15 years. For more than half of that time I was director of ministry, first on the *Logos* and then on the *Doulos*.

When I tell people about our experiences, most of them assume that I was the captain. While the captain operates the ship as an ocean-going vessel and has full authority to which all crew members submit, as director I led the on-board community and the ministry. I often compared my responsibilities to those of the pastor of a local church – except that I lived with my congregation seven days a week and even had breakfast with them every day.

The OM ship ministry focuses on the local churches in each port. In contrast to regular ships that are in port for as short a time as possible, our ships took shorter voyages and spent longer periods in ports to develop relationships with local believers.

While our emphasis was on the local churches on shore, we did also function on board as a church. If the essence of church is based on the truth that 'Where two or three come together in my name, there am I with them', then we certainly were church. For this is the *sine qua non* of what we are all about. Jesus' presence among us makes all the difference to who we are and what we do in the places we travel.

Each staff member and volunteer on board is sent by their local church. The three hundred people on *Doulos* at the time came from over 35 different nations. So we truly represented the church universal. Our unity in diversity, in fact, was one of our most striking testimonies – such unity encourages and convicts Christians and non-Christians alike.

'You're just like the United Nations', said the president of one country about *Logos*, 'but the one difference is that you are united!'

'As soon as I stepped on board, the one thing that struck me most was the unity among the people represented on this ship. If people of 35 nations can live, work and serve together, I cannot see why people of Sri Lanka cannot get along together in a much larger space!' said the Honourable G.L.B Hurulle, Minister of Cultural Affairs in Sri Lanka in 1998.

The apostle Paul said that we are members of one body and that we should exercise our God-given gifts to build up the body and function in service and ministry to one another and to others (see 1 Corinthians 12 and Ephesians 4).

One of the most striking lessons I learned in leadership on the OM ships centres on this truth. My function as director (pastor) was not so much to be the directive 'boss' but to facilitate 'body' functioning. The more I directed my energy into this aspect of leadership, the better we functioned as a community and the more fruitful the ministry. Conversely, we functioned less well when I took a more authoritarian position in leadership. Leadership does entail making difficult decisions, but most often I was able to facilitate team building with other leaders and the 'body'.

Some of our most wonderful memories are of our regular (weekly) times of extended prayer together. We were often tired after a hard day's work, but our energy picked up as we met with God and poured out our hearts to him in worship and intercession. And we saw God's power in action in so many ways. When local authorities in Venezuela closed down the *Logos*, we prayed. An hour's prayer time extended through the whole night as we were convicted of wrongful attitudes in our hearts. God brought conviction and repentance and a victory when the ship was re-opened a few days later.

Our fellowship on board was rich, and relationships grew deep as we shared with and cared for one another. We understood that we needed one another – and we couldn't run away from each other. A ship is restricted environment with real physical limitations. Each person's weaknesses quickly became obvious. Broken relationships had to be faced, and we learned to practise forgiveness and reconciliation. We had a taste of what the church in Acts 4 must have been like.

Jesus said, 'By this all men will know that you are my disciples, if you love one another' (John 13:35). The more we demonstrated this love, the more powerful our testimony was – much more powerful than all of the organized conferences which are, of course, vital to the ministry but become a 'resounding gong' without love.

An individual's own spiritual growth is an integral part of the ship experience and is in fact one of the motivations people have for joining the mission, so this aspect of 'church' receives a good deal of attention. Opportunities for growing in this way present themselves daily on the ship. More than skills, we learn how to relate and function together, how to understand and accept one another. Inability to do this is one of the reasons for missionary attrition, and the breakdown of personal relationships is also at the roots of many church splits and divisions.

In all of this, the Bible is our foundation, our inspiration and motivation for the life we live and the service we offer. It is not a set of guidelines and principles but our daily bread from God himself. Personal as well as community devotional times are part of the rhythm of life on the OM ships. Individuals spend time reading and studying the word of God and fellowship and Bible study groups meet regularly. We pray always that the word activated by the Holy Spirit will speak into our personal lives and into our community life.

The leadership on the ships provides spiritual eldership, grounded in the word and exercised under God's authority in the 'church'. This also gives the right and the basis for discipline to be administered. If the leader does not operate from this foundation, his discipline becomes misdirected and can degenerate into abuse. The leaders, therefore, must be living their own lives under the same authority.

What role did the sacraments play in our church on board? We broke bread together during our community fellowship and prayer times, but not usually on a Sunday morning when we encouraged people instead to visit local churches. We did not practise baptism on board because we came from different denominational persuasions and, out of respect for our home churches, we advised crew members to consult their home churches in this matter. When an individual felt God was leading him or her to take this step, we encouraged contact with a local church to ask the pastor for baptism.

Our policy was to voluntarily lay aside areas of denominational doctrinal differences and controversial practices for the period of the person's commitment. We in no way insinuated that these are unimportant, but we emphasized the more fundamental (and numerous) areas on which we all agreed. This policy enabled us to focus on our common calling to the Great Commission.

My time on the OM ships was among the richest and most deeply rewarding experiences of living as the body of Christ, of what church really is all about. We can't live on a ship forever, and sooner or later we all live on land. The challenge for those who have the opportunity to live on a ship for a time is to bring the principles learned on board into our on-shore churches. Because life on board is compact and intense, this is not always easy. But living and being church is our goal – on land and on sea.

7

Seafarers are Longing for a Church

Seafarers on the oceans the world over are longing for a church. To give you a taste of this yearning, following is a letter sent by a Filipino seaman to my co-worker Volker Lamaack:

> Thanks to God for giving you always time for serving us. I hope and pray you'll continue your mission as long as we live. Very truly, we seamen greatly need people like you. People who have the courage to preach the word of God and our Lord and Saviour Jesus Christ. You know very well about our lives as seamen. Sometimes it's very hard for us to avoid temptations. All these things block our way to God. It seems like we are living in a different kind of world, a world far away from God, a world abnormal in nature. We cannot attend Bible seminaries when we need it. We cannot go to church when we need to go there. We cannot hear the word of God preached by somebody like priests or pastors or ministers. We cannot participate in Holy Masses during Sundays and holidays. Sometimes we even forget it is Sunday. There are times of loneliness, being far away from home and families for so long. Sometimes we don't have the emotional support from our families when we need it the most. There are times of boredom especially during long voyages where you can't see something new. Everyday you can only see the same environment, your ship, the sea, waves, cloudy skies, same faces. That's why some people said, that we seamen are very much the same as prisoners. And yes, it's true, we are prisoners confined in one ship, where we cannot do anything we want to do..... There is no true freedom. All these things are very hard to cope with when we don't have the strength and guidance coming from God. It is through God's grace that we are able to survive our job.

Yet many of us are on the wrong way, a way which leads farther and farther away from God. We always sin against God. And that's why we need help. Please help us to pray and ask for the forgiveness of our sins. Thanks to God, that you continuously look for those lost souls and bring them back to God. I hope and pray that God gives you more power and strength as you continue your mission throughout your lives.

Another letter from a seafarer expressed this longing for a church in this way:

I like to be in the church. Here is where I feel the presence of our Lord. And that is what all seafarers are missing after having a long contract on a ship. They even start to forget the church because they have been away from it for so long.

On a large container ship I met with several seamen from the Pacific island state called Kiribati. After having lunch with them I had the opportunity to share more about Christ and the need to accept him as personal Saviour and Lord.

'Where will you go when you die?' I asked them. 'To heaven or hell?'

One of the seamen did not hesitate. 'I would go to hell!' he said.

Although I was a bit taken aback by his straightforward answer, I was glad that he did not fool himself as many do, saying something like, 'Well, my good works are more than my bad works, so I suppose God is pleased with me and he'll take me into heaven.'

'Do you really mean that?' I asked him. 'If so, why are you so sure?'

And this answer surprised me even more than his first.

'Because I have no church,' he said. 'I have to sail so many months on a ship and cannot go to church. That's why I believe I'm going to hell.'

I spent a lot of time with him, trying to explain to him that he still has a chance to go to heaven even if he is sailing many months on a ship without seeing a church. At least I had the opportunity to clarify the gospel for this man. But this man said what many seamen think. 'God cannot be pleased with me because I never visit his church.' This sort of reasoning, of course, stems from a wrong understanding of salvation – that enough good works, visits to church and trying your best will please God. Many people, seamen among them, have this magical notion of church – that we can please God simply by entering his church, even if we are not willing to think about, much less obey, God. And so my prayer is that God will save men on these ships so that they can start churches that will teach truth and be vessels for transforming lives.

I will never forget one Filipino seaman, a dedicated Christian who was working on a general cargo ship. His ship sailed from England to Hamburg and was staying in Hamburg for three days, which is an unusually long stay. When I visited that ship on Monday I met this man, and he told me that he was very disappointed that he had not been able to go to church in Hamburg the previous day. It had been over six months, he told me, since he had been able to visit a church. He was the only Christian on board his ship and he longed for Christian fellowship. I apologized that he did not have a chance to visit a church, but I did not know of his ship sailing to Hamburg because the missionary in the last port had not informed me of his coming to Hamburg. It was difficult and painful, in the face of this seafarer's disappointment, to explain that missionaries often have limited opportunities to bring seamen to our churches.

Another Filipino seafarer with a Roman Catholic background wrote the following letter.

> I like to stay in different churches in different places. I like to stay inside the church for a couple of minutes, because when I am inside I really feel the presence of the Lord and that is what all sailors are missing when they have a long contract on board a ship.

On another occasion I received a letter from an Indian seafarer who came with his ship to Hamburg and had a deep desire to visit a church. Unfortunately, I was so busy on other ships that day I could not bring him to church. At that time I was still the only port missionary in Hamburg and some 60 ships were in the port every day. A fine Christian on one small tanker wrote to ask me to come and teach them the word of God, because the port stay of his ship would only be a few hours.

Many sailors over the years have expressed their desire to visit a church. In a survey of five hundred seafarers, many indicated that one of the highlights of their seafaring time is when they have a chance to worship God with local Christians in different countries. We have had wonderful times of fellowship over the years when seafarers have been able to visit our churches. After church we often sit together and talk, laugh, pray or play. We have received many letters from seafarers expressing their gratitude for taking them to church. Often there is language barrier and our visitors are unable to understand anything from the sermon in German, but they feel at home among us. They are grateful to feel that sense of belonging to the house and family of God.

One time, when a Nigerian sailor visiting our church was giving his testimony, I was concerned when he said, 'If you have a problem just look to your hand and your problem will be solved.' What kind of strange theology was this? As I was translating for him, my mind was racing. What should I do or say to correct this? But then he told us that the reason we are to look at our hands is because our five fingers stand for J.E.S.U.S. In other words, just look to Jesus with your problems. Needless to say, I was very relieved.

Since shipping has become much faster, however, we have found it increasingly difficult to invite as many seafarers to church. Since many seafarers have a strong desire to be in church, and since some actually forget to visit churches when they are home and have the opportunity because they have gotten out of the habit during their long periods at sea, I encourage them to make every effort to communicate with their home church. Some do, and it means so much to them when they receive letters from their pastors. Some churches even send tapes so seafarers can listen to the preaching of their pastors. Occasionally churches even send Bible study materials which seafarers can then use on board ship if a church is started.

While the following prayer of a Filipino seafarer does not explicitly speak of his longing for a church, one can read between the lines to see how important a church for such a seafarer would be.

Lord please be there when we need most a guiding hand and watchful eyes, light our ways from every port amidst the freezing cold of winter. Strengthen our hearts every moment when our ship rolls like a tin can, when the wind blows with rage. Give us your aid every moment and keep our tired engine steady. Show the path our ship should sail, keep us all away from danger. Keep us all to love your name. Grant us, Lord, a gentle wind for us to reach the shore again. Amen.

Over the years we have received lots and lots of letters, faxes and emails in which seafarers have expressed their joy about having a Christian meeting on board their ships. Usually they refer to these meetings as Bible studies or Bible sharing times, occasionally Bible teaching. When I ask more about these meetings, however, it usually becomes apparent that they meet as a church even though they do not call it church, perhaps for some of the reasons we have discussed above. They come together regularly to sing and praise God, share testimonies, pray for each other and listen to God's word. We are often asked to supply Christian resources (Bibles, tracts, concordances, hymnbooks, etc.) or to pray for them. Here is what one seafarer, Captain Renato S., wrote:

Good day Brother Martin, how are you today? I guess it is more than a year now since the last time we met when my last ship, *Lowlands Yarra*, discharged at Hamburg. The last time you visited you gave us a Bible study booklet written in Tagalog titled 'Ang Tulay'. We are using it now during our Bible study every Sunday and the crew is learning a lot from it. Thirteen crew are regularly attending and we have nearly completed the whole study book. Could you please send us the next study book to continue our Bible study? We would appreciate it very much if we could receive it at our next port in Constanza, Romania.

I spoke with Captain Renato several times on the phone, and he told me that the number of people who studied God's word grew even bigger until they finally went home. When Captain Renato came back to the ship after his vacation he immediately started to teach the crew God's word. They now meet again every Sunday, with about 12 people building each other up in the faith.

Captain Cirilio P. from the Philippines wrote the following email:

> Good day, please be informed that we have a Bible study every Sunday on board and we would like to ask for a Tagalog Bible and hymnbooks. Before we start and close our Bible study we sing Christian songs. Our goal for our church is to preach the good news to everyone to know and believe in HIM. We started the church on board when the chief engineer and myself talked about a Bible study and we asked the crew if they would attend if we met on Sunday. God is the one who gave us his gifts to use in the church … to evangelize, teach, preach and share the word of God. We have two elders on board.

Communications such as this and the following, from Ritchie B., are so encouraging and give a glimpse of the power and joy of God's church on the oceans:

> Well, about the church on board, we started it the last Sunday in May after we left our last port in Europe, which was in Le Havre, France. It is doing great! We meet regularly every Sunday evening about 6 o'clock after we have eaten our dinner. Our meeting lasts for about one to two hours. It is sad to say, that not all of us are there because others are on duty when we meet. We still pray for them. On behalf of the ship I would love to say thank you for all your encouragement you have given us.

8

Seafarers who are Disappointed and Hiding from Church

While there are many seafarers who are longing for fellowship and would love to experience church on board, there are also those on ships who have mixed feelings about church. They might even have once been eager to attend meetings with Christian content but due to present circumstances are now hiding from any kind of Christian contact. I have met many people who have shared in private conversation that they have accepted Christ but for one reason or another do not want to attend church on board. For some it is only a legalistic matter – they would attend if the church on board practised exactly as their home church did. God is not pleased, they reason, unless the format and doctrines fit their precise denominational formula. Others are young converts who are afraid of their non-Christian mates and therefore would rather act in a way that seems not too 'spiritual'. The largest group of seafarers who do not attend church on board, however, as far as I can see, are the 'backsliders'. Even after they have come to me and confessed that they are backsliders, they still find it difficult to start going to church. One reason for such behaviour, especially among people from Asia, is their so-called shame culture.

The worst thing that can happen to an Asian is to lose face. On the huge cruise liner the *Queen Mary 2* I have met Christians from China, Indonesia, India and the Philippines who have never yet attended church on board. While some did have to work during the church meetings, the majority did not go because they were ashamed that they had backslidden and were hiding from their Christian brothers and sisters. While I was sitting in a mess room on the *Queen Mary 2*, one Filipino Christian approached me and confessed that he really needs church but had never attended because he felt so low spiritually. When I encouraged him to start going to church every Saturday he agreed that was a good idea, but I could read in his eyes that he was not too sure. People's fear of the opinions of others is so strong. When a Christian knows that others have seen him doing things a Christian is not supposed to do, he cannot face the person who saw him. I once met a young Christian seafarer who was tempted by a prostitute. When he realized that I knew his situation, he would not meet me again. Others who have been seen drinking or dancing in bars hide away, feeling they have denied the Christian faith.

4. *Queen Mary 2* – a huge ship with more than 1200 seafarers on board, but no church yet

How can these men be brought back to the church on board? Often they need wise counsel and understanding. They need to know that Christ, as their intercessor, is still there ready to forgive. Such situations often present perfect opportunities for port chaplains, as neutral and objective third parties equipped to listen and teach gently from the word of God, to talk with these burdened seafarers. Because seafarers trust and respect port missionaries, we can often bring these backsliders back into the ship church. Port chaplains in this pastoral role pray for much wisdom to use these opportunities for the glory of God. If these backslidden seafarers are restored, God will use them mightily on board and also in their churches at home.

9

The Social Aspect of Church on Board

Seafarers have little freedom and few social contacts. Their jobs do not allow them to achieve what others on shore assume is normal. Most people, for example, are able to meet with friends, neighbours and relatives – in our own homes, in theirs, or in any number of places. Seafarers do not enjoy that privilege. Most of us are able to have social contacts and a social life on our own terms, but seafarers cannot choose their friends or social activities. They work, confined on a single ship, for up to a year or more. Then they have a break of a few months or, if there is an emergency, a break of only three to four weeks. Some journeys from port to port take as long as 35 days – during which time they don't see other people or other countries. They see the same faces and the oceans. Some seafarers have likened the life on board to life in a modern prison. After their daily work, they are often tired and go to their cabins to rest. Many times they do not even meet with others on board because they are tired and also because they have problems that they are afraid to share with each other. Life often gets boring. Many seafarers on cruise ships work under deck all day and seldom see the daylight. Some get depressed and lonely and feel very isolated.

All they have to look forward to is enjoying themselves in the next port. They like to meet with people and make friends ashore. They like to see new cities. But with all the problems in today's world, sometimes seafarers are not allowed to leave their ships when they arrive in a port.

If, for example, they sail from Hamburg to Columbia to load bananas there, the company asks them not to go ashore because of the dangers in Columbia. So they stay on board, hoping that in the next port they might get ashore. But if they sail next to the United States, for instance, they might find it difficult to go ashore because the US has tightened their security since 11 September 2001. Several seafarers have told us that they were not allowed to go ashore in the US. Seafarers might sail to three or four ports there without being allowed to go ashore, and so frustration quickly sets in. Even if they are allowed to go ashore at a given port, there are often delays that require the crew to work overtime and so they are not able to leave the ship due to lack of time.

For many Asian seafarers, Asia was always a good place to go. They could often meet relatives working in different port cities and enjoy time in a culture similar to their own. With the advent of SARS in 2003, however, shipping companies no longer allowed seafarers to go ashore in Singapore, Hong Kong, Shanghai, Taiwan and other cities. In other places ships don't even go into ports for fear of pirates. This is the case, for example, in Nigeria, where many ships load or discharge cargo miles away from the port area.

It is not inaccurate, then, to say that the ship can feel like a 'modern prison'. I have met seafarers who did not leave their ships once during their entire ten-month contract. Visitors such as the port chaplain, therefore, are all the more welcome on board ships. But I have seen the tremendous difference a church on board can make. Meeting together regularly for church provides the social contacts seafarers miss during their stay on board. Some seafarers do not really know each other until they meet regularly in their ship church. Here they can share their problems, their fears, their loneliness and their difficulties with people. Here people will care for them, will pray for them and will help them in practical ways as well. Here they can laugh, relax and enjoy fellowship. It is amazing that even the Japanese shipping company of the *MOL Integrity* noticed the positive atmosphere on the ship because of a church on their vessel. A church on board will definitely bring a spiritual change, but it also brings a social change. Some seafarers will, for instance, stop going to doubtful bars, getting drunk and hanging around with girls.

Where seafarers do not meet together, I have seen the opposite effect. Often crew members on these ships run to their own cabins after work and have very little contact with one another. The atmosphere on the ship as a whole is usually very different and is often very depressed. Sometimes huge problems arise between the seafarers themselves. I have witnessed many a fight on board ships between seafarers who simply did not have the emotional and physical strength to endure ten months away from home. Ten months isolated.

But I have also witnessed the real help, encouragement, mutual understanding and healing of division that a church on board can bring. If seafarers come together for prayer, worship and Bible study; if they pray for each other and carry one another's burdens; if they experience healing for their souls and bodies – then they will go home after their contracts and be able to testify to what God has done on their ships, how God solved their problems and touched them personally and met their every need.

10

Guidelines for Planting a Church on Board

During the last ten years or so, I have met many seafarers who have had both the maturity in their faith and the gifts to start a church – but who have not, for various reasons, taken the step of planting a church. I have put together some guidelines, therefore, for seafarers and missionaries who would like to plant churches on ships.

One Filipino engineer told me that he felt he had the knowledge to start, but because the seafarers were so far away from God he didn't know how to start. And so the first, and most important, guideline is prayer.

1. Pray

Psalm 127:1 says that 'unless the Lord builds the house, its builders labour in vain'. We must carefully prepare the foundations of churches on ships with prayer. We come to the Lord and give him our hearts so that he can fill us with wisdom, understanding, love and patience. We must never forget that we are not the church builders – the Holy Spirit is. And it is Christ who is the head of the church (Ephesians 1:22).

2. Make friends and lead them to Christ

Often the most effective approach is to bring just one friend to faith. Train this friend in the word of God, meet with him as much as you can and let him watch your life with Christ. I began to meet with one such friend, Saroh Diaz, each time his ship was in port. I made a special point to sit down with him to get to know him better and give him a chance to get to know me better also. We went through a lot of questions from the Bible together and, after several Bible study courses, he gave his life to Christ. I then took time to disciple him more and pray with him. I brought him into contact with other port chaplains who gave him more training, encouragement and prayer and we encouraged and motivated him to start a church – and he did.

3. Bring the believers together and give them a vision

One of the saddest things I have seen on many ships is that there are believers who hide their faith. On the container ship where Saroh Diaz came to know the Lord, I met with other believers as well, who at first were quite shy. Going through some Bible study courses together revived their faith such that they felt equipped to share their faith with others on board. I reminded them that they are not seafarers only but, first of all, ambassadors for Christ (2 Corinthians 5:20). When we met together as a group of believers we talked about the meaning of church and its multiplication and shared the Lord's Supper together. We also talked about how it would be their task to plant churches on other ships as well. I was so excited when I saw the second officer of that ship starting a new ship church on the next vessel he worked on. The same happened with other believers. Whenever they had a vision, they went home with the vision and returned to a ship in order to live that vision.

4. Share the vision of ship church with your home church

Seafarers as well as missionaries who board the ships need to share this vision with on-shore churches. It is important for seafarers to be able to share their questions, disappointments, duties, challenges, joys and blessings with their home churches. In this way their home churches can take part in the church planting process. This collaboration will bring blessings to the seafarers as well as to the home churches. Missionaries should also share the vision of planting churches with their own church fellowships. These are perfect opportunities for local churches to take responsibility in prayer and practical duties to encourage and build up ship churches.

5. Build a strong relationship between the port chaplains and seafarers

It is vital that chaplains and seafarers work closely together and establish good communication links. These contacts can now be maintained through email and SMS text messages as well as the telephone. The port chaplain can provide Christian material to the ship and can also help in many practical ways. He can relay prayer requests from the ship churches to the many individual Christians and churches who have a burden for seafarers. Seafarers should call, write or phone the port chaplain as often as possible so that the port chaplain will know how he can best help. It is important that the seafarers inform the port chaplains about changes on board and also about changes of the route.

6. General things to observe

It is important to have a good sense of the ethnic and religious backgrounds of the seafarers. It might be necessary to train Christians how to approach Muslims, Buddhists, Hindus and people from other religions in a tactful way. Secondly, it is important to observe the general atmosphere on board and to learn if seafarers ever attended church on other ships. It is also essential for those wishing to start a church to know how many believers are on board. If there are several believers, it is best to begin meeting with these believers to pray together so that the Holy Spirit can unite them for planting a church on board. Practical considerations such as scheduling (so as to avoid as much as possible conflicts between church times and working times) and where to meet also need to be decided. Usually it is wise to let the captain or staff captain know about the desire to form a church on board.

11

Examples of Church Planting from Ports around the World

Hamburg, Germany (Martin Otto)

Because Hamburg is a huge container port ships come back quite regularly, and this is an advantage for ministry among seafarers there. In shipping language there are the terms liner shipping and tramp shipping. Liner ships always follow the same route, whereas the routes of tramp ships are always changing. One of the liner ships that visits Hamburg every two months is the *MOL Integrity*, a container ship with about six thousand containers' loading capacity. When I first visited this ship I did not know anybody on board. So I began to share the gospel with the Filipino crew through a series of short evangelistic sermons using lots of illustrations. After giving such a message I would ask the seafarers if they would be interested in studying a Bible correspondence course. I was surprised and delighted that about ten seafarers on the *MOL Integrity* took a study course and started to study the Bible with great zeal.

Two months later, when I saw the ship again, several seafarers gave me their test papers from the completed course. So I gave them more study material and, before long, Saroh Diaz realized that he needed the Saviour and gave his life to Christ. I noticed changes in him from the very beginning. When I saw how Saroh loved the Bible and how intensely he studied it I encouraged him to start a church on board his ship. He hesitated at first – I think he was fearful of what others would say. After we finished reading a book called *Personal Evangelism* together, however, he

was absolutely convinced that the Lord wanted him to start a
church on his ship.

We prayed about it and, when the ship finally came back to
Hamburg on 20 November 2002, I was greeted by many of the
crew with great excitement and joy. They told me that they had
started to meet every Sunday for Bible study and, to my surprise,
the attendance was very high. There were 17 Filipinos working
on the ship, and 16 attended the first meeting. Over the following
weeks the attendance averaged between 12 and 14. The number
would have been even higher but for the fact that some could not
attend because they were working from 8 p.m. to 12 a.m. Most
probably the attendance was so high for two reasons. First of all,
Saroh was a good example of what it means to be a Christian
who loves Jesus. People on his ship had seen his change in heart
after he came to know Christ as his Saviour. Secondly, almost all
the crew had already started a Bible correspondence course and
thus were prepared when Saroh invited them to church.

These Bible correspondence courses, which we ordered from
Emmaus Bible School in England, are instrumental in creating
a desire for more spiritual things. Another man who was saved
through these Bible courses was Vitorio Eliseo, a young seaman
who worked in the engine room. He used to drink a lot and many
people testified how much he had changed since he accepted
Christ as his Saviour. We saw similar changes on other ships.
When people studied Bible courses they also wanted to attend
church, whether or not they had accepted Christ yet.

On the *MOL Integrity* they met every Sunday. If for any reason
they could not meet on a Sunday they changed the meeting to
Monday. Their meetings were very lively. Although they did not
have a guitar, they would still sing. They wrote down the words
to songs from a Christian worship CD and sang with enthusiasm.
Through the Bible study courses Saroh came to realize that
baptism was a step of obedience that Jesus was asking of him,
and so he asked me if he could be baptized. 'If only the ship had
a bathroom', he said, 'then you could baptize me there.'

It is amazing to see how God used, and continues to use, a
seaman who had only been a Christian for nine months and who
has no theological training. Saroh has a deep love for Jesus, for
the people on board and for the Bible. I had the privilege of going

on board and talking to them in depth about the importance of church and its meaning. In the evening, after their day's work, we met together and shared the Lord's Supper. They so enjoyed this, and it was the first time some of them had experienced communion. Tears of joy were shed. They are eager to continue to live church on that container ship. During our meeting we prayed that God would provide a new 'pastor' to replace Saroh when the time came for him to leave the ship. God immediately answered that prayer and sent another dedicated Christian, Deo, a third engineer who also had a vision for church on the *MOL Integrity*.

5. Aboard ***MOL Integrity***, part of the church that was started through one faithful Filipino

After a time, Saroh was honest enough to admit that he felt the burden of being a pastor on the ship was too heavy for him. So when the ship returned to Hamburg in May 2003 I talked to Deo and asked if he would be willing to act as pastor. Without any hesitation, he said 'yes'. He had a sense that the Holy Spirit was calling him to lead the church. Together with the crew, we appointed Deo through prayer as the leading elder on the ship.

Although there was a higher ranking officer on board who also belonged to the church, he was humble enough to admit that it was the right decision to appoint Deo as an elder. Saroh and the rest of the crew promised to encourage and support their new pastor in his new role leading the church.

I was tremendously blessed to hear about the impact this little church of about 14 people already had. The Japanese shipping company had noticed a big change in that the crew were no longer drinking alcohol. The company was also surprised to see how well the crew members worked together. Deo also told me how they had experienced an amazing answer to prayer. A seaman had come to them with overwhelming pain in his chest. The church people prayed for this man and, immediately afterwards, he testified that his pain had disappeared completely.

The *MOL Integrity* was unique in that they had more than one port chaplain who visited the ship. Rudy Kuijer in Rotterdam and David Thomson in Southampton, who are on the staff of Seamen's Christian Friend Society as well, also went on board to encourage these men in their faith. Follow-up in other ports is crucial. If we want to have strong ship churches then we need to make sure that missionaries in the various ports of the world visit these churches to encourage and equip them. Temptation and discouragement can so easily set in if these churches and their members are not supported.

Rudy and I experienced a similar situation to that on the *MOL Integrity* on the container vessel *Al Mutanabbi.* The crew consisted of about 16 Filipino crew members, some Indians and Pakistanis, one Syrian, a few from Iraq, one Maldivian and eight Egyptian officers. The chief cook Voltaire Narvasa, who came to know Christ through reading a New Testament that was given to him by a port chaplain in Houston, Texas, was eager to share his faith with his colleagues. Immediately after he began work on board he invited people to come together and meet for fellowship, Bible study and prayer. There were four at the first meeting, eight at the second. The last time I heard, their regular attendance was up to 13, including two seamen from India.

On his own initiative Voltaire started a school of discipleship every Wednesday. The experience of having started a church motivated this man so deeply that he felt guided through the

Holy Spirit to invite his Muslim superiors to special services at Christmas and Easter. At this Christmas service he testified to what Christ did for us all. To his surprise, every Muslim and Hindu who attended the meeting enjoyed it, and the captain told some of the seafarers that he was sure Voltaire was a messenger of God. They hope to be able to invite some of these Muslim and Hindu crew members to church.

It is always amazing to experience the different spirit on such ships when there is a church on board. You can almost feel the presence of God. This positive atmosphere encourages other seafarers to visit these ship churches just because they are curious. They want to know why their ship mates have changed so much. They also want to experience this peace and joy in their own hearts. These churches, like the ones on *MOL Integrity* and *Al Mutanabbi,* are a tremendous shining testimony to Christ. Seafarers who are not Christians witness the peace, understanding and community among the Christians. Often the Christians do not even have to preach the gospel – their lifestyle draws others to learn more about Christ.

Yet another example of such a ship on which God has done amazing work is the *Goonyela Trader.* I met the captain last year and had a good time of conversation with him. I gave him a Bible study correspondence course in Tagalog, his native language. He brought the course along with him to his next ship, where he studied the course with his crew. He sent me a fax message to say that 15 people meet regularly every week for Bible study and prayer and requested more Bible study books for his crew.

To give a better flavour of what life is like in these ship churches, below are first-hand accounts from Saroh Diaz, who started the church on *MOL Integrity,* and also from the chief cook who started the church on *Al Mutanabbi.*

'MOL Integrity' – Saroh Diaz

I write this to share with you our wonderful moments on board with Christ. On 6 October 2002 our first Bible study was conducted on our ship. About 15 people gathered in the mess room. … There was a sudden change of atmosphere and it was a strange event for the unbelievers. Some were glad and eager to join us while others were reluctant to hear the good news. But for me it was a very special day, because God allowed it to happen in spite of our situation on board. God gave me ample courage to fight the fear of future difficulties, criticism and other hindrances that lingered in my mind until I first experienced this real joy on board with Christ.

I was not a real Christian and was not faithful to the Lord before I joined that ship. I thought I really knew him, because I had been zealous as I was growing up in my traditional religion. I used to observe and obey every activity and celebration of this belief, although the doctrine was not based entirely on the Bible. I observed the law of God carefully. I tried to do good to others and rendered proper respect to people. I did all this expecting to gain righteousness through my own efforts. But indeed I was blind and absolutely wrong. Perhaps this was due to lack of knowledge of the word of God, which is the word of truth. During this time I believed human doctrines instead of the doctrine of God.

In May 2001 I started on the ship as a deck cadet after three years of study and two years of training. I got to know the life of a seaman, which is very difficult – far away from home, no time or very limited time to go ashore in port, very risky work. When we had bad weather at sea I was like a drunk man vomiting all day long. My first experiences were very bad, but I endured all these agonies and eventually started to embrace this profession I had chosen.

When we made our maiden voyage and arrived in Hamburg, the first missionary who visited us was Martin Otto. He gave me the correspondence course called *The Bridge* and I learned a lot of spiritual values that were unknown to me before from Martin. Some crew members, including myself, received Bibles. Martin spoke to us about the Lord Jesus Christ and helped us to understand more about him. One can learn so much about God by opening your heart to this wonderful message.

In my free time throughout our long voyage I started to learn and read the Bible because at that time I was still unfamiliar with it. I also studied *The Bridge*, and its clear illustrations helped me to understand a lot about what the Bible teaches about Jesus Christ. … What a saviour for seafarers like me! Every time we were in Hamburg Martin was there to help us and lift up our spiritual life in Christ. He was also kind enough to help us by mailing letters from seamen to their families. He gave us several spiritual books which helped me to read the Bible diligently – although not every day, due to our irregular schedule of rest and work on board. The more I read the Bible the more I liked it, and I slowly began to understand the truth of who Christ really is. I discovered the meaning of his life, death, resurrection and ascension to heaven. For the first time, I was serious about spiritual matters. My mind slowly renewed and I focused on him and his promises like the one in John 1:12: *'to all who received him, to those who believed in his name, he gave the right to become children of God'*.

After finishing several Bible correspondence courses and reading several books that Martin gave me, in addition to reading the Bible itself, I noticed that my thoughts really changed. I accepted the Lord Jesus into my life. I knew that I had found the truth and was amazed by the gospel of grace given to me from God. Even my work performance improved – to the extent that my chief officer appreciated my work in a way he did not before. When I encountered any problem on board or even from home, I went to the Lord in prayer and trusted Jesus to help me and resolve the problem.

In September 2002 we were in Hamburg. Martin came to visit us as he always did. But this time he encouraged us to have church on board. I know that most of the crew were not in favour of that because they were thinking of all the various difficulties such as lack of time, the criticism of others, insufficient knowledge of the Bible, and different religious practices. But I was convinced that if we studied the word of God daily with an open heart and mind, and with the Emmaus correspondence courses, we would be able to share properly the word of God with others. Before Martin left the ship that day, he gave me a green book called *Personal Evangelism*. He prayed with me and encouraged me to start the church on board with weekly Bible studies. To my surprise, the second officer told me that he was a Christian too and he also encouraged me to start the Bible study. Although I thought it was a good idea, I didn't feel ready to take that responsibility.

While we were on a long voyage I gained new confidence to take that responsibility. *Personal Evangelism* gave me ideas for evangelizing the crew. When I finished the book I decided to start the work as Martin suggested. I told the second officer, who was very glad. That very day, while most of the crew was dining, I announced that we would have a Bible study at 18:00 hours in the crew lounge and that everyone was invited. Most of them were surprised. Then I hurried back to my cabin to prepare ... I prayed that Jesus would help me to deliver his word fearlessly in front of my fellow workers. After praying I went to our meeting place and, in front of my fellow workers, I delivered the word of God seriously and honestly. This was the first time in my life I spoke openly before others. I was a little nervous, but I knew that Jesus was in control and that he would help me to make it better the next time.

I noticed that most of my fellow workers did not know how to find a passage in their Bibles. The second officer and second engineer, who was also a Christian, spoke from the word of God to the crew as well. As we shared God's word, I noticed that some of the crew were laughing, some criticizing and opposing because of different religious attitudes. Those who were eager to listen to the word of God could not concentrate. Those who opposed us strongly believed in their own traditional beliefs instead of the Bible. After two hours, our first Bible study finished. As I went back to my cabin I heard that some wanted to continue every week and I was overwhelmed with joy. The following day one seaman approached me to say that he had been praying that one day there would be a Bible study running on the ship. God had answered his prayer. Some crew told me with amazement that this was the first time they had experienced such an activity on board a ship.

* * *

As our Bible study continued week by week I used my free time to prepare my topic from the Bible with some ideas and illustrations from the Emmaus Bible correspondence courses. One of our crew, who was newly baptized, gave me a small booklet that taught the principles of soul-winning step by step. There came a time when I felt too tired and discouraged to continue this spiritual work on board. Possibly this was because others criticized me and I felt the enemy trying to hinder our church activities. My work as a seaman, however, was not affected – in fact, I gained more discipline. Despite the difficulties, I upheld the word of God and stood firm in Jesus who is able to give us the strength we need.

One day we learned that our third engineer would be replaced, and we felt sad about this. At our next gathering as a church, however, the new third engineer attended. When he testified to what Jesus had done in his life, I was surprised and glad. I had never expected that he would know the word of God. This new third engineer, Deo Lachica, told us that he was supposed to join another ship, but God led him to work on our ship. Certainly his presence with us was part of God's wonderful plan for him and for us. Deo had never experienced this kind of fellowship on board before, and he was eager to continue this. He told us that he used to preach in his home town and that he wanted to grab the opportunity with full confidence to testify about our Lord Jesus Christ before the other men on board. I appreciated his God-given knowledge every time he helped me when I did not know how to explain from the word of God. He is a mature Christian, and we are so glad that God sent him to our ship.

When our ship returned to Hamburg, we met Martin again. He was overjoyed when we told him about our gathering every week. As usual, he brought us many wonderful spiritual books and encouraged us to continue with the church. He also gave us contacts for missionaries in Rotterdam and Southampton who were able to encourage and teach us more. In addition to meeting our spiritual needs, all of these missionaries in Hamburg, Rotterdam and Southampton also cared for us practically by providing such things as winter caps, gloves and woolly hats and by mailing our letters. We were so grateful for their kindness and care. One time our chief cook forgot to order sugar for our ship. He discovered this after our departure from Rotterdam. The chief cook told me about the problem and that his Japanese superiors were very sensitive about the matter. Our next port was Hamburg, and I told him that Martin might be able to help. We arrived at 5 a.m., and at 8:30 a.m. Martin arrived, promising us that he would bring the necessary sugar in the afternoon, which he did. We were so grateful that God had used Martin to free us from this worry.

Through the blessings and strength that he showered on us, God had made it clear that I should continue our Bible study on board. Our weekly gathering had become a real church. We began with a simple prayer, offered songs of praise, read and explained the gospel and, before our closing prayer, we sang praises to our Lord again. Even our captain at that time and our Japanese principal were glad when they heard about our weekly gathering and they, too, insisted that we should continue.

Our church on board is now eight months old and growing. While at first we gathered in informal clothes, now those who attend dress nicely for the glory of God. Martin and most of the church brothers appointed Deo as the elder of the church, and he is now acting as our pastor. We rely on our Lord Jesus, no matter how big or small our gathering. Some have left the church without telling us their reasons, but we are confident that God will enable the church to grow.

Below are a few of the things that we have experienced as a church on board the *MOL Integrity:*

- Our church donated some money towards building a Christian church in the Philippines. The letter asking for this help came from the wife of one of our fellow crew members who is involved in that church.

- One of our crew members suffered a skin infection that spread quickly over his body. Deo led us in a time of prayer for him, and God answered our prayer. After only a few days he was completely healed.

- One crew member became a Christian through our church. He had been a heavy drinker and a slave to different kinds of vices. He abandoned all of these for Christ's sake and we heard recently that he and his wife were baptized during their vacation in the Philippines.

- After the second officer who started the church with us on *MOL Integrity* went for vacation, he returned to work on another ship called *MOL Solution*. He started a church on this ship because he had found so much encouragement through church on board *MOL Integrity*.

- In June 2003 we received a guitar through Mr Martin Baker, who visited us in Southampton. He also gave us several worship, praise and song books.

I share all these things to testify to the great power of our Lord Jesus Christ. Without him we can do nothing.

'Al Mutanabbi' – Voltaire Narvasa, chief cook

Before joining my next ship I prayed to the Lord to send more believers on board with whom I could have a team ministry on the ship. I believe that seafarers who are believers really need a church on board ship. Church on the ship is a continued service to God while we are far away from our homelands. If there is a church on the ship we can continue in worship, fellowship, prayer, teaching God's word, breaking of bread and evangelism. Just as when I am at home, personal communication with God is not enough for my spiritual life and growth – I need church as well. To be away from our loved ones for nine months is not an easy life. The life of a seaman is sometimes like a prison if you are on a long voyage. In port many temptations are always present. A church on our ship gives us strength to overcome temptations, to help each other, to comfort and encourage. The church helps us to become 'overcomers'. Our church on board the container vessel *Al Mutanabbi* started in November 2002 when I boarded the ship. I immediately invited seafarers into my cabin for Bible study. At first there were three seafarers who accepted my invitation and we met together as a group of four. The next Sunday God added three more seafarers from the deck department to our church. The believers in our church enjoyed our meetings so much that they invited more seafarers, and finally we had 13 seafarers regularly attending the church meetings, including two Indian seafarers. Since my cabin could not accommodate that number of people we transferred the church meetings to the crew's mess room. We usually meet on Sundays from 8:00 p.m. to 9:30 p.m. We start with praising our Lord. After that we pray and invite others to give testimonies and express their gratitude to the Lord. Then we read the Scripture text for the evening, followed by the message. After the preacher has finished his message everyone is given the opportunity to ask questions regarding the message. After this time of questions and answers everybody is encouraged to share prayer requests. Following a closing prayer we enjoy a time of fellowship while we prepare food. Finally we partake of the Lord's Supper, the breaking of bread.

Every Wednesday from 8:00 p.m. to 9:30 p.m. we have a school of evangelism, in which I train the people to be able to share the gospel of salvation with others. This also involves discipleship training. Everybody who comes along is given the opportunity to practise what he has learned and to demonstrate the gospel. I have two mature Christians with me who are able to share the gospel and who are also feeding the young converts. We always write everything on a sketch board, which helps them to visualize and digest the material. Once or sometimes twice per week we also meet in my cabin for prayer from 5 a.m. to 6 a.m. There we praise the Lord and have a short message as well.

On two occasions so far we have invited everybody on the ship to participate in our Sunday meeting. All were invited at Christmas and I was able to share why Christ was born into the world. At Easter we invited all of the people on the ship again and everybody attended, including the captain with his wife. There were Muslims, Hindus and Christians at the meeting. I had the privilege of sharing Christ and explaining that he is the only way to be saved.

I believe that any seafarer who is a believer could start a church if he has the right biblical message and if he is sure of his calling of God to share Christ on the ship. According to Matthew 18:19,20, church can start with two or three. God will add more people. I have sailed so far with Hindus and Muslims from India, Egypt, Pakistan and Iraq. They knew what I was sharing with them and they were never disturbed by it. In fact, some of them even joined the fellowship.

One important link for our church is the relationship we have with my home church in the Philippines. Once a week I call them and share what God is doing on the ship. I ask them to pray, and they promise that they will do that. They also share with me what is happening back home, and we as a church on board pray for their requests. This relationship helps to keep the church on board alive. We also pray for other ship churches that have been established.

Montréal, Canada – Hans Uittenbosch[15]

6. The author preaches in a church on board a bulk carrier

On almost all cruise ships there are small Christian fellowships or Bible studies, usually arranged by a few very positive evangelical Christians. They generally meet in groups according to nationality because of the language problem. They meet in different areas, sometimes assigned by the crew-purser. Most of them meet late at night, between 11:30 p.m. and 2 a.m. and last about an hour or longer. Someone takes the lead to open the meeting, and either himself or someone else brings a message. The musical aspect is lively, spirited and inspiring. The Indonesians on Holland America ships meet ecumenically, and their gatherings are more like formal worship services. On some ships there may be as many as four or five different groups. On only a few ships have I discovered the participation of Caucasian Christians. But in ten years I have never seen an exclusively Caucasian Christian fellowship. Most groups are small in number – between five and twelve people. On some ships, like the *Norway* and some of the Holland America Line ships, Indonesian groups are larger, between 25 and 45 people. On Holland America Line ships, the Protestant pastor is ordinarily asked to present a message

---

[15] Rev. Hans Uittenbosch has served among seafarers in different ports of the world and has also served as a sailing chaplain on cruise ships.

at the fellowship hours, but in many cases they are unable to make contact with the Protestant pastor. I have made it a point to personally inspire the pastors to take the lead. For most ships' chaplains, doors plastered with signs including 'Private', 'Crew Only' or 'Officers Only' are enormous barriers and prevent meaningful contact. Once the contact is made, crew really appreciate the distinct biblical messages that chaplains present to them. On almost all ships, a priest comes to give mass to the Roman Catholics crew members. Although an occasional Caucasian is found amongst them, the majority of attendants are Filipino. The presence of 'Christianity' or 'religiosity' or 'spiritual awareness' is often measured according to the number of Filipinos on board. The meetings are normally advertised in the crew quarters. The posters are not very inspirational for non-Christians, and I have spoken to a number of the groups about the best ways to draw some of the non-Christians to their meetings. This coming Sunday I will lead one of the Christian fellowships which currently has five members, including one recently converted Christian girl from Australia who works in the spa. She has not only joined the group but is nearly leading the group, for which we praise the Lord.

Alaska, USA – David Hawkins[16]

The Alaska Christian Ministry to Seafarers has helped many groups get started on the passenger ships. I refer to these groups as Christian Fellowships Aboard (CFA's). There are, of course, many other groups we've encountered that were formed before we knew them. There are three distinct, yet overlapping, aspects of our ministry to the CFA's. These are: 1) planting; 2) equipping and encouraging; and 3) shepherding.

1. Planting

It seems best to illustrate with an example of one of the fellowships that was started by our mission. When I first visited the *Universe Explorer* in 1997 there wasn't a CFA. I sought permission to hold a nondenominational church service aboard each time the ship

---

[16] David Hawkins is a member of the team at the Alaska Christian Ministry to Seafarers, which visits seafarers on cruise ships in Alaska.

visited Seward. This was granted and I was told that I could use the crew mess room for the purpose. For six years Betsy, our guitarist, and I would go aboard and minister to the crew with a one-hour service. We took song sheets with us, in English, Spanish, Tagalog and Indonesian. At the beginning there was a core of believers among the crew, and we encouraged them to start a fellowship. This they did with some success; however, when the ship returned the next year the group had stopped meeting. The brother who had been the leader wanted to pass the responsibility on to someone else. No one came forward, so it was a full year before another leader was found and the group started meeting again.

Please note: finding a leader is always the first step. I often refer to Isaiah 6:1-8 when encouraging the faint-hearted to take a leadership role. People often have the idea that they need to have been to seminary. The first step a man of faith must make in this direction is to put up a notice to say that there will be a Bible study, with the time and place clearly shown. Sometimes the staff captain will allow the group to use the PO's mess room, or some other place; otherwise it has to be held in a crew cabin. What matters, and what needs to be emphasized, is that the faithful need to be meeting together as a body, regardless of denominational backgrounds. I always tell them that they are the 'aroma of Christ' in the cruise ship industry (see 2 Corinthians 2:15).

Back to the *Universe Explorer* ... the fellowship has been solid now for the past three or four years. One interesting thing in all of this is that because of our association with HIM (Harbour International Ministries),[17] I contacted Kurt and Thea in Cape Town two years ago and asked them to visit the *Universe Explorer*, which was about to spend a couple of days there. They said they would do this, so I emailed the security officer aboard and arranged for them to go aboard. The ship has been there about four times since. Now whenever the ship is in Cape Town most of Kurt and Thea's church, including the choir, visit the ship for a service on board. The captain has also given the group permission to hold services along with the passengers. It should

---

[17] HIM is an international umbrella organization for many evangelical seamen's missions.

be pointed out, however, that the *Universe Explorer* is a college ship when she is not in Alaska.[18]

2. Equipping and encouraging

Over the years we have been able to locate sources to provide us with Bibles and quality Christian materials in many languages. We provide these to the various groups on ships without cost. We encourage the members to write to us for whatever they need, even when the ship they are working on does not visit Seward. We simply mail what they need to the ship's agent in whatever country they will be visiting. Sometimes we are able to put the order on a ship that comes here; it then gets passed on to the ship it is intended for at a port both ships are visiting, thus saving on postage costs. As mentioned above, encouragement is also an important part of preparing willing spirits.

3. Shepherding

It should be remembered that many of the seafarers we work with are in Seward on a regular basis. Some we have been seeing for up to 20 years. This helps to give us some credibility. The reason I mention this is because when divisions within groups start to appear, we are able to guide and direct without appearing to be interfering. Incidents of division have always occurred when a leader seeks to promote the particular doctrines of his own church too vigorously. We have seen examples of this with regard to the charismatic style of worship, the question of baptism, eternal security and women pastors. The important point is to convince the seafarers to avoid any extremes – they should focus upon what they agree upon – their Savior and what he did for us.

Singapore – A vision of the port chaplain Werner Strauss[19]

From Singapore, one of the largest ports in the world, I received an article with the following headline:

---

[18] Instead of having regular passengers, so-called 'college ships' have college students taking courses at sea for which they earn credits. These courses are accredited and the teachers are fully qualified.
[19] Rev Werner Strauss is a port chaplain with the international Lutheran Seafarers' Mission in Singapore.

MINISTERING SEAFARER PROGRAM WITH EMPHASIS ON DEVELOPING CHRISTIAN FELLOWSHIP GROUPS ABOARD SHIPS AND NETWORKING WITH OTHER PORT CHAPLAINS

I am privileged to share with you the 'ministering seafarers program', the goal of which is to find and help seafarers to be ministering seafarers – MS for short – on board. The emphasis is on developing Christian fellowship groups and follow-up ministry with other port chaplains. I did not start this program or the follow-up ministry but tell you about it in the name of the many who do it. This program began in the nineteenth century. Through the distribution of Bibles and other Christian literature, hundreds of cell groups were organized on ships and expanded rapidly. The ministry launched their own emblem in 1817, the so-called 'Bethel flag'. It was hoisted on the main masthead as a call to worship. With increasing secularization, it disappeared in the middle of the twentieth century. Is it mad to dream that the flag will fly one day again?

Why should we try to find and help seafarers to be ministering seafarers aboard ships and to start fellowship groups?

1. They need a viable Christian community right in the place where they work and live so they can survive as Christians. Very often seafarers have to live without Christian fellowship for quite a long time. (I know from conversations how lonely seafarers can be and how desperately some search for spiritual fellowship.)

2. I am limited as a chaplain in terms of the service I can offer, because ships are in port for such a short time.

3. To enable seafarers not only to receive the gospel, but also to be its messenger in witnessing to their fellow seafarers.

4. I believe that the spiritual and social input a ministering seafarer contributes will help to improve the conditions on his ship.

The MS knows better than anybody else what life is like on board and how to reach out to his fellow seafarers. My job is to take the opportunities I have to develop and encourage the growth of

MS positions and, through them, the establishment of fellowship groups on board.

The ultimate goal of having an MS on board was to have a church on board. The port chaplain in Tacoma, Washington, USA, had the goal to see a church on every vessel by the year 2000. Although that goal has not been reached, that should not stop us pursuing the goal to have a church on every ship. Here is what the former chaplain in Tacoma said: 'We give follow-up literature to at least one person on the ship. He becomes a "ministering seafarer"', he explains, adding that this seafarer can then distribute literature to others on the vessel. 'This program is one of the most promising signs that the goal to see "a New Testament church with a viable witness on board every ship crossing the oceans" may be more realistic than some observers might think.'

Sydney, Australia – Rob Flinders[20]

P&O Nedlloyd Los Angeles is a ship with some Filipino believers on board, and I wanted to talk with these men about the idea of beginning a Bible Study fellowship on board. I asked our supporters to pray for Tyrone and the other Christians on board, that they would begin meeting together regularly and that they would reach out to the other men on board by inviting them to join their group for Bible study. *MSC Japan* is another ship that has two Christian Filipino seafarers on board.

In June, both *P&O Nedlloyd Los Angeles* and *MSC Japan* were in port on the same day. So we invited the four Christians from the *P&O Nedlloyd Los Angeles* – Tyrone, Loreto, George and Ferdi – and the two from the *MSC Japan* – Lito and Arvelito – to come to our home in the evening for a time of fellowship and encouragement. Cynthia and Lito, our Filipino brother and sister in the Lord who live nearby, and Lewis and Jeanette from our Bible study group, also joined us. Altogether twelve people were present, representing five different countries – the Philippines, Malaysia, Singapore, the Netherlands and the United Kingdom.

---

[20] Rob Flinders is a port chaplain with the Seamen's Christian Friend Society.

We sang gospel songs and prayed together. We also spent some time investigating what the Bible teaches about church and how that could be applied to their circumstances on board ship. I shared with the men some practical ways I thought they could put this into practice. We were all blessed by our time together.

P&O Nedlloyd Los Angeles arrived back in Sydney on 22 July. When I went on board, Tyrone, Loreto and Ferdi greeted me with huge grins and the announcement that they had some good news for me. They whisked me off to Tyrone's cabin, sat me down and gave me a blue folder containing a sheaf of papers and a number of photographs.

When I opened the folder I discovered that every Sunday evening for the five weeks since the ship was last in Sydney, they had held a church service in the crew recreation room, between 8:00 and 9:30 p.m. The papers in the folder showed how they had collectively planned these services and how they had allotted specific responsibilities to different people to lead the singing, to lead the prayers, to read from the Bible and to deliver Bible messages. The extent of their preparation was extraordinary.

So, too, was their initiative and commitment to make these meetings successful. They showed me a host of songs they had neatly written out on poster-size sheets of paper so they could be pinned up on the bulkheads in the recreation room, big enough for everyone to read and sing. They also showed me two tambourines that they had manufactured in the ship's engine room from copper piping and steel washers. These two tambourines, together with a guitar, provided the musical accompaniment for their singing.

They also showed me the content of the Bible messages that different people had prepared for each week. One of these was called 'Worship'. Another was 'The Church' and another 'Salvation'. In their service in the fourth week they celebrated the Lord's Supper using ship's biscuits and orange juice. The message for the fifth week was entitled 'How to Pray' and had been taken directly from Lesson 7 in the Emmaus course entitled *Spiritual Milk for New Believers*. I was encouraged that they had used this material, which I had recommended to them because it would enable them to deliver sound teaching and reinforce individual Bible study.

The folder also contained a record of the names of the men who had attended each service. Between 11 and 14 men had attended the service each week – these numbers would have been a great encouragement to all of them, and especially to those who worked so hard behind the scenes during the week preparing.

In the photographs they showed me I saw the men gathered together in the ship's recreation room as 'the church on board *P&O Nedlloyd Los Angeles*'. The photos clearly show their sincerity and their joy.

As Tyrone and Loreto and Ferdi shared excitedly about the past weeks, I realized that some, if not all, of the men had been affected in different ways by what had been happening with the ship church. Tyrone, Loreto and Ferdi were convinced that God had been at work amongst their ship mates as they praised him in song, talked to him in prayer and listened to him as the Scriptures were read and preached. I shared in their joy and excitement and thanked God with them not only for what God has done and is doing, but also for what God will do through and among these men in the future.

Eventually each one of these men will finish his contract and return to his home. In due course each one will join a different ship. As they do, they will take with them their first-hand experiences of starting and running a church on board *P&O Nedlloyd Los Angeles*. They have seen it happen and they have seen it work. By his grace God might use some of them to help establish church fellowships on board other ships amongst other men. What has happened on board one ship could be multiplied by three or four ships and 40 or 50 men – or more.

Tyrone also told me that the men had collected US$200 to purchase an electronic keyboard to use in their worship services. They were hoping to make this purchase before the ship sailed, and Tyrone's chief officer kindly gave him the following morning off from work so we could look for one. Ian, one of our prayer partners at Mascot Fellowship who also plays the keyboard in our church services, spent some time on the internet and located a few second-hand keyboards for private sale in not-too-distant parts of Sydney. I made some telephone calls and identified two that might be suitable.

Tyrone and I set off on our search, and in the providence of God we had procured a keyboard by midday. The story is remarkable. One of the keyboards was about a 15-minutes drive from Port Botany. The other was further afield, in the northern suburbs of Sydney. We decided to try the closer option first. This keyboard turned out to be exactly what the men on the ship were hoping for. It was a Yamaha, less than a year old, in perfect condition and hardly used. The owner still had the two instruction manuals and also his receipt showing he had purchased the keyboard brand-new for $399. He was willing to sell it to us for $275 Australian. Tyrone and I talked it over and we decided to buy it, so I paid the agreed price. With the keyboard and accessories in the back of the car, Tyrone and I drove to the bank to convert the crew's US$200 into Australian currency so that I could be reimbursed. We received $271 Australian!

There was great excitement when we arrived back on board the ship with the keyboard. The men crowded around, eager to see and hear, and in no time at all one of the men, an accomplished keyboard player, was playing it. He was clearly delighted, and so was everyone else.

It was a blessing to be able to help these men and to share in their excitement. As I pray for them now I can imagine them singing on Sunday evenings, accompanied not only by a guitar and homemade tambourines, but also by a keyboard. I was again reminded of Jesus' words, 'It is more blessed to give than receive.'

12

*What Seafarers Think about a
Church on their Ship*

I asked different seafarers who are leaders of churches on their ships to conduct an informal survey among the crew regarding their views of the church on board. The questions I gave them were also in part to assess whether there is a need for a church on board ships. These seafarers were more than happy to answer several questions and even added some of their own. Although some were even a bit critical, the majority liked the idea of having church on board. These are the questions that I asked:

a) Do seamen need a church?

b) Would a church on the ship make your life on board any different?

c) Is it possible for seamen to start a church on a ship?

d) Have you experienced church on a ship before?

e) What are the difficulties starting a church on a ship?

f) If you have experienced church on your ship, what did church life look like?

g) In your opinion, what is a real church?

h) How can a port chaplain help to start a church on a ship?

Following are excerpts from some of the fascinating replies I received.

Michael S. is a Filipino Christian currently sailing on a cruise ship. He is leading and teaching two groups of believers. Here are some of his thoughts, which he permitted me to pass on:

> I handle two groups – one local and one international. When I say 'local', I mean a group that belongs to my ethnic background. So we have fellowship and study in our own language. Do we have church on board? Sort of...though I do not claim to have all the necessary gifts for the ministry. I am just glad that the Lord allows me to lead a small group of believers. Of course there are plenty of 'professing' believers on board, and since we are a cruise industry we (the crew) represent 80 different nationalities from all over the world. But in reality only a handful of us continue in fellowship. We pray that the Lord will add more souls to the kingdom through us – this is where I need more prayer. The only thing I have not done is to conduct regular communion. I am also praying that one day we can have regular worship services on board. Currently I am the leader/teacher and often even the song leader as well. Ship life is a lot different than land life, as you might know. All activities on board have to be patterned to set time frames of the day. Freedom is defined a bit differently, on top of that are thousands of policies, rules, training to attend.... Please pray for more effective ministry on board our vessels. I am just one of the brethren doing the same: earning a living and trying to spread the good news. After all, Paul was the model tent maker. You will wonder what we do with our day off – well, we don't have one. We work mostly 12 to 14 hours every day. Some work even longer hours than that. I do not call myself a missionary; I do not feel worthy of that honour and do not have the training and resources. I am just content being a worker where God assigns me. Thank you for taking the time to get in touch with me and share your thoughts and concerns about the ministry. Thank you for working and helping to further the cause of the kingdom. I would be delighted to hear from you again.

And from Bruce M., Australia:

> Dear Brother Martin, Thank you for your enquiry. Personally I have to answer a 'No' to most of your questions. I find it very difficult on Australian ships to implement on board ship church

due to being the only Christian most of the time.

There is a suggestion I do have, however: Five years ago my family and I went on a South Pacific cruise for 13 days. We noticed a great need for on-board chaplains on cruise ships, regardless of company or nationality. We sailed with P&O and found the need great. Please keep in touch with me, won't you? I would like to keep in contact with you, bye for now.

In Christ,

Bruce M.

From Ramon S., Philippines:

Seamen need a church on board. It will help every individual to grow spiritually and it will create a harmonious relationship on board. It would really make a difference in everyone's life as in times of trials, problems and temptations there always would be someone to help and to advise. I believe if there are only two believers it is possible that they can start a church if they have enough courage. On my present ship, however, the captain did not allow us to meet. We already started church and had the joy to see six people accepting Christ as their Saviour. Later one of the seamen was talking behind our back to the Captain and spread some lies so that the Captain stopped our meetings. The evangelical port chaplains are a big help to us. They not only bring material but also spiritual blessings. We experienced that through Rudy Kuijer and Martin Otto. Because you helped us in practical ways the seafarers on board stopped thinking that born-again Christians are strange people.

From Adam R., Philippines:

Often the seafarers are neglected by the nations and the church. The word 'church' refers to a local group of believers (Philemon 2). So here are the answers to the questions: Seamen first need a chapel in their heart and after that a church on board. Yes, the church will make one's life different if it is established on board ship. As we know, the very purpose of the church is to worship God and to glorify him on earth; to evangelize the whole world with the gospel; to teach and instruct and to witness constantly (Acts 1:8). … I have experienced a church on board. But sometimes it is difficult if leaders on the ship do not permit us to meet with others for fellowship. It is also difficult if you have to move every time you meet from one place to the other. In this situation the port missionary played a big role when he came on board to encourage and counsel us. In my opinion, we Christians are the church called out from the world's system to be in Christ. In 1993 I was on board a ship with 21 crew. The captain was holding mass but the seafarers only attended because the presence of all was forcibly demanded by the captain's power. When I joined the ship I first cleaned my cabin from all sorts of posters, crosses, pornographic magazines and seductive newspapers. I prayed: 'Lord, you brought me to this vessel because you wanted it. You are my Master and I am your servant. Command me and I will do.' I started a church on board and 16 seafarers were attending. We all enjoyed the presence of God and worshipped him. We even had drums on board made out of empty plastic detergent containers. We met every Wednesday, Friday and Sunday. It was really a church, to God be the glory!

One of the seafarers who attends a church on a container ship answered the questions as follows:

Do seamen need a church? Because the ship is our community, it is necessary for a ship to have a church. We engage in physical activity in the course of our daily work. Likewise, we need to develop our spirituality through reading the Bible together with fellow workers. Most seafarers spend almost a year on a ship, so it is best if they spend that time worthily in God, with a family of believers.

Would a church on the ship make your life on board any different? Through a church on board we can practise a brotherhood in Christ. While we imitate Christ's attitude we develop spiritual and moral values. Through church our faith abides in Christ, and our hope is renewed every time we come together. People who attend church will slowly realize the truth and abandon their immorality while at the same time walking towards God. Broad knowledge about God can slowly be obtained as the word of God is expounded by someone who is knowledgeable enough.

Have you experienced church on a ship before? No, I haven't – perhaps due to a lack of true believers on ships I've worked on, and maybe also due to the fear of difficulties.

What are the difficulties starting a church on a ship? Lack of courage. Fear of negative feedback from others. Fear of not being able to explain why a church is needed. Fear of different religious practices.

How can a port chaplain help to start a church on a ship? By providing us with spiritual books, magazines and most of all the Bible itself as well as free Emmaus Bible correspondence courses that helped us to draw nearer to God. The port chaplain can also encourage those who are weak in faith. We received strong support from port chaplains, who urged us to build a church of God on our ship.

7. The church on the *Royal Princess* that met at night because there was no time to meet during the daytime

Yet another seafarer answered the question concerning the difficulties when starting a church on ship as follows. 'Some captains did not allow us to meet. We also lack Christian literature, especially the Bible.' The same seafarer also answered the question about what church life on board looked like: 'We began by sharing the Bible with others and we studied God's word together. When we had three crew members regularly coming we made it a habit to meet weekly. We also had a weekly prayer meeting and a time of worship in which we sang and praised the Lord. In this way other crew members were encouraged in their faith and others joined us. We were able to bring some to the Lord Jesus.'

I was also struck by what another seaman said when he was asked about how a port chaplain could help in starting a church. 'Most of the time the seamen will not listen to their fellow seamen if we are sharing Christ. Yet there is a much greater chance that they will listen to the port chaplain when he comes on board to share Christ with them.'

13

Starting, Growing and Multiplying Churches on Board

Biblical criteria for starting a church on board ship

In the New Testament, the word 'church' is a translation of the Greek word *ecclesia*, which means 'a called out people, a gathering or an assembly'. It has often been said that the church is not an organization but an organism – it is not a lifeless institution but a living unit. It is a fellowship of all those who share the life of Christ, and who are linked together in living union by the Holy Spirit. The church is God's masterpiece, an object lesson to principalities and powers in heavenly places of the manifold wisdom of God. Every believer should therefore be vitally interested in the church – even in churches on board ships.

As William McDonald says in his book *Christ Loves the Church*:

> We believe that the New Testament approach is this. All believers are instructed that, by the grace of God they are members of the church. They are exhorted to gather together in such a way as to give expression to the great truths of the church. The language of the scriptures is the language of grace; namely 'You as believers are the church, now meet in such a manner as to give an accurate expression of this fact to the world.'[21]

When we think about starting churches on board, we need to think about practical considerations as well as the spiritual or

---

[21] William MacDonald, *Christ Loves the Church* (correspondence course from Emmaus Bible College, USA), chs. 1, 2.

biblical criteria for a church. While this division is helpful in terms of breaking down all that needs to be considered, some practical points will overlap with the spiritual and vice versa. As we have seen from Matthew 18:20, a church is only possible when there is more than one person. Church is always plural – people are meeting to worship God. This, therefore, is as much a practical point as a scriptural one. God makes it clear in the Bible that he desires leadership in his church, and this is only possible if there are at least two or three people at the absolute minimum. Practically speaking it will not be easy to have a leadership that consists only of two people. However, Jesus Christ promised that he will be in their midst. So if a seafarer is the lone Christian on a ship and is sharing Christ in meetings that others attend I would call it a Bible study group or fellowship group. But when people come to know Christ as their Saviour then leadership can start. Biblical tasks can be delegated and a church can begin. A church on a ship has four main points of focus, as mentioned in Acts 2:42-47:

> They devoted themselves to the apostles' teaching and to the fellowship, to the breaking of bread and to prayer. Everyone was filled with awe, and many wonders and miraculous signs were done by the apostles. All the believers were together and had everything in common. Selling their possessions and goods, they gave to anyone as he had need. Every day they continued to meet together in the temple courts. They broke bread in their homes and ate together with glad and sincere hearts, praising God and enjoying the favour of all the people. And the Lord added to their number daily those who were being saved.

These were the pillars of the early church and these are still the pillars of our church today. All of those I have talked with from church ships have affirmed that they practise these: first, teaching (the doctrines of the apostles); second, fellowship; third, the breaking of bread; and fourth, prayer.

Hebrews 10:25 is also very important for the situation in which Christian seafarers find themselves. 'Let us not give up meeting together, as some are in the habit of doing, but let us encourage one another – and all the more as you see the Day approaching.' As we have seen, Christian seafarers suffer because they feel as if they have given up their church. While they have a strong desire to worship God in the body of Christ, they have had to leave their home churches for work on a ship. Seafarers are always having to give up meeting with their church at home. The writer of the book of Hebrews warns us not to give up meeting with the believers in church. Is that warning not true for seafarers? Does it mean that seafarers are disobedient for leaving their church? Do they have to fear punishment for leaving the church? What are the practical consequences seafarers have to face after they have left church in their home country? These are some of the questions that Christians on board ship ask.

But the church can be anywhere. Jesus Christ, the head of the church (Colossians 1:18-19 and Ephesians 1:22-23), wants Christians everywhere to worship him. He does not limit the church to certain buildings or even to the land. Because Christ loves everybody the same, every Christian should be able to worship God in a church. Seafarers who are Christians only start to feel guilty when they do not meet together as a church on board. I have visited many ships where there were several Christians on board who did not meet for fellowship, prayer or praise. Hebrews 10:25 has a message for them: 'Do not give up meeting...'

In 1 Peter 2:4-5 we read: 'As you [seafarers] come to him, the living Stone – rejected by men but chosen by God and precious to him – you also, like living stones, are being built into a spiritual house [church] to be a holy priesthood, offering spiritual sacrifices acceptable to God through Jesus Christ.' The idea of building here supposes a work so wrought that souls become conscious of forming part of the dwelling place of God, and are rendered able to offer up spiritual sacrifices as a holy priesthood.

In 1 Corinthians 14:26 we read about orderly worship in the church: 'What then shall we say, brothers? When you come together, everyone has a hymn, or a word of instruction, a revelation, a tongue or an interpretation. All of these must be done for the strengthening of the church.' And so these things must also be done for the strengthening of the seafarers. This is exactly what seafarers need. There is no reason why this could not be seen on a ship.

In the New Testament we see that churches need a strong leader with a vision. The apostle Paul, for instance, had received excellent teaching and was able to pass on to the churches the things that he learned. So before we start a church on board we must make sure that the seafarers receive solid biblical teaching. Secondly we must find, through prayer and personal conversations with believers, a person who has an apostolic gift. I usually meet with such a person several times on the ship or in our home before I encourage him to start a church. Often seafarers do not feel adequate for the task of leadership aboard. An excellent passage to share with him would be Isaiah 6:1-8. When Isaiah encountered the vision of God, his sin became all too apparent. Even so, after his sin had been removed, he said to God: 'Send me!'

I have noted that the people who have such an apostolic and prophetic gift (Ephesians 2:20) are usually very well accepted by the other crew members. This seafarer also needs to have a passion for a church on his ship. Once that person has started a church, we try to discern who among the group has which gifts. On one ship in particular I met with the seafarer who started the church on board and, at the same time, with one other person who has shepherding gifts. Through these people, I am able to teach the whole church. While I also meet with individual members of the church to talk and pray, I focus on the leaders. My priority is to train them so that they have a burden and vision for even more ship churches. We as missionaries want to bring the gospel through seafarers to the farthest corners of the earth. When there is an established church on board, its members can do an even better job of preaching Christ to the unreached in other ports and to their ship mates. They know the context and the people better than we do, and they also have more time. 2 Timothy 2:2 is a key verse: 'And the things you have heard me say in the presence of many witnesses entrust to reliable men who will also be qualified to teach others.' The goal is to entrust God's powerful word to reliable men, who then will be able to teach their ship mates. And these ship mates will find more people they can teach, so that they in turn will be able to teach still others. If the process of discipling and teaching is ongoing, we will see many ship churches in the future.

One practical thing that often helps ship churches to get started is a library. I always encourage seafarers to contribute the books they purchase and read to build a small library, rather than these resources being the property of individuals. In this way the resources do not go home with the seafarer at the end of his contract while the group is left without. Church offerings that are collected can be partly used for these purchases as well, and also for acquiring musical instruments. One of the effects of this practise is to give a greater sense of permanence to the church on board.

Denominational affiliations should be avoided. The point is not to build a pentecostal, Anglican, Baptist, Methodist or brethren church. The point is to build churches on ships that glorify God and that multiply. I have witnessed many problems resulting from seafarers insisting on following the particular practises or preferences of their denomination. This creates tensions among ship mates and does not help them to grow in faith and spread the gospel to others – on the ship or with others in different ports. Fights for particular names or denominations have resulted in churches never being established. I am convinced that the devil is using this question of denominations to bring disharmony among Christians on board ships.

I once visited the *Queen Elizabeth 2* and was asked by one of the church leaders on board if I could teach them the word of God. So many denominations were represented among them that these differences had caused problems in the ship church. I was asked to teach, and not to preach, as they wanted to know what the Bible says – and not what one particular denomination says.[22] I am glad that the Bible doesn't give us church names, but only the names of cities where the churches were located,

---

[22] In this context we need to identify the difference between preaching and teaching. When a seafarer listens to preaching, his experience is often that the preacher is either seeking to convert the listener to a particular denomination or is only putting forward his own particular slant. In other words, many preachers limit themselves to a narrow range of subjects to win people over to their particular point of view. When a seafarer asks for teaching, what he really wants is good solid broad teaching from the whole word of God. This will help him to strengthen his faith and grow in discipleship.

for instance the church at Ephesus or the church at Corinth. I have always strongly encouraged leaders, therefore, not to give the ship church a particular name. We usually just call it the church, and everybody on the ship knows what is meant by that. Sometimes people call the church by the ship name, for instance 'MOL *Integrity* church', but this has never led to confusion. One of the keys is to encourage seafarers to have a balanced Christian life and to not overemphasize their church convictions from home churches. If we created a new denomination, then seafarers could go home with the intention of starting the same sort of church at home – and this could also lead to divisions. I am also convinced that it is easier for Muslims, Hindus, Buddhists and those from other religions to accept a church on board without a particular name.

Spiritual growth of ship churches

It is one thing to start a church, but it is another for it to grow and multiply. As we have seen, a church on board ship is necessary for Christian seafarers to grow in their faith. But a church on board faces special challenges in terms of growth. Since seafarers are home for such short periods of time, for example, they sometimes do not have a deep or mature understanding of what church is all about. It is occasionally difficult to help seafarers understand that churches should grow in the knowledge of our Lord Jesus and that churches should also fulfil the mission command of Jesus found in the Gospels and also in the book of Acts. Seafarers also often need to be taught about what it means to have a calling to be ambassadors for Christ (2 Corinthians 5:20). The very transitional nature of their lifestyle, while it has its advantages, can also inhibit sustained Christian growth within a body of believers. While some of the teaching of the ship church will be quite basic in this respect, no church should feed its believers 'milk' all the time. These churches need strong spiritual food which will enable the seamen to witness for Christ and to be seen as a testimony for Christ. There are several key ways to ensure that the church that was planted grows in grace and knowledge.

First of all, as we have seen, the church needs the right spiritual food so that they can live by it and can grow themselves.

The believers should have a clear sense of the purpose, goals and vision of their church. The Bible correspondence courses we have mentioned throughout this book help individuals to grow in their faith, thereby strengthening the whole church. Some of these courses cover the basics of what church is all about and how church is to be a place of God's people worshipping God. This understanding is foundational for seafarers to make church growth a reality. Besides Bible correspondence courses, there are many good books and preaching tapes, videos and DVDs.

Some churches (on shore and also on ships) do not grow for the simple reason that the members are not balanced in using their gifts. There may be a church that has several teachers but no evangelist. Or they might have an evangelist but no shepherd. Maybe there is an apostle and a prophet but no teacher and evangelist. The Bible teaches clearly that God wants different gifts represented in his church. The book of Ephesians 4:11,12 describes these gifts: 'And he gave some, apostles; and some, prophets; and some, evangelists; and some, pastors and teachers; for the perfecting of the saints, for the work of the ministry, for the edifying of the body of Christ' (King James Version). Especially on ship churches with their limited numbers, this ideal constellation of all five gifts (apostolic, prophetic, evangelistic, pastoral and teaching) hardly ever occurs. It is therefore important for ship churches to receive maximum input from outside. If a ship church has only two or three of these gifts, missionaries visiting this ship in ports might have the additional gifts and thus be able to equip the church to do what God has appointed it for.

Without input from the outside it will be difficult for a ship church to have a balanced church life, and especially when the ship church is small (only three to five people, for example). Communication between missionaries concerning which ship churches are lacking which gifts is therefore vitally important. A good follow-up system will give these newly founded churches the best support to grow in grace and knowledge to the glory of God. Developing relationships between several ships and/ or shore churches would also serve to strengthen the existing churches on ships. A church on shore could take responsibility for a ship church by praying for them regularly and also by teaching them from the Bible, encouraging them, and even offering training – through emails, faxes or even letters sent by post. Churches on shore, who could act like mother churches, could be a tremendous encouragement to churches on the oceans. I have seen this sort of relationship in action, usually when the home churches of seafarers have been active in teaching their members. In the church on board *Al Mutanabbi,* for example, the chief cook who acts as an elder of that church phones his home church once a week and shares everything that is going on on the ship, including prayer requests. It is important for home churches to play an active part in strengthening their members in their faith in Christ. It is equally important for seafarers to maintain close relationships with their home churches. Port missionaries can act as mediators between the churches on shore and the churches on the oceans.

Radio ministry has been a very fruitful method of ministering to churches on the oceans. The Seamen's Christian Friend Society (SCFS)[23] in the Philippines, for instance, has a ministry to seafarers through radio. Many seafarers hear the word of God on the radio while they are sailing on the oceans and are encouraged in their daily walk with the Lord. The director of that radio ministry in Manila, Mr Vic Atanacio, also writes letters to encourage seafarers, especially Filipinos.

Another very important aspect of the ministry to seafarers and churches on ships is the ongoing pastoral ministry that David Thomson, seamen's pastor with the Seamen's Christian Friend Society, is involved in. David writes regular pastoral letters to the believers on ships. This correspondence enables him to encourage and inspire the seafarers in their walk with the Lord. David shares spiritual input in teaching and counselling with seafarers which they appreciate very much. Seafarers know that they can ask David any question, and he will answer their letters and try to help wherever possible. Once the contract of a Filipino seafarer finishes, we put him in touch with Vic Atanacio and his co-workers in the Philippines. Vic and his team do everything possible to make sure that the seafarers find solid, mature churches in their various home towns in the Philippines.

---

[23] An evangelical Seamens' Mission based in Manchester, England that was founded in 1846 with missionaries in several countries of the world.

Vic is also actively involved in discipleship work and he has often had the joy, as a result of discipling the seafarers and their wives, of seeing whole families come to a saving knowledge of the Lord Jesus.

Multiplication of ship churches

Jesus is very clear in the Bible that we are not to make converts but disciples. A Christian should not live on his or her own but should be a disciple – telling others about Christ and multiplying the body of believers. We also see this concept in 2 Timothy 2:2: 'And the things you have heard me say in the presence of many witnesses entrust to reliable men who will also be qualified to teach others.' In the same way, and by God's strength, we are to multiply churches. It is not enough that one seafarer starts a church. Those who start churches need, at the same time, to seek and pray for people to train who will then be able to start churches on their next ships. Only in this way will churches on ships multiply worldwide. This training will cover study of the Bible as well as practical advice. This is what the chief cook Voltaire Narvasa did on his ship *Al Mutanabbi*. First he started the church, but then he identified some motivated Christians and taught them how to witness for Christ and how to grow as disciples. These were not just theoretical lessons. They put what they learned into practice on board ship. He trained three seafarers and met with them for prayer every week. I am convinced that these three people will have a passion for church on their next ships because they have seen the beautiful testimony and vision of their church leader.

On the huge passenger ship *Jewel of the Seas*, which employs 928 seafarers from 62 different countries, a small church has been established. Just imagine what an impact this church can have, reaching 62 nationalities on just one ship! What missionary can reach so many nationalities in such a short time? Imagine what could happen if this church gives a clear vision of church planting on ships to all the believers on board. When these believers take that vision on to their next ships, the idea as well as the reality of church on ships will multiply.

8. *Jewel of the Seas* – A cruise ship with more than 900 seafarers from over 60 different countries

One other seaman I met trained people in his church in evangelism and asked them to invite unbelievers to evaluate and give feedback on their testimonies. While they judged the testimonies they would, at the same time, hear the gospel being explained! I have met seafarers who started planting churches without having been trained through other seafarers. These men came from home churches where they were taught God's word in depth so that they were mature enough in faith to be able to start a church. Other seafarers who want to start churches on board simply follow the example of fellow Christians whom they met on their last ships. Some seafarers live their faith in such a practical way that others watch, learn and follow in their footsteps to start churches on other ships. Starting a church without formal or intentional training may not always be the best or easiest way, but when people fall in love with Jesus, the Holy Spirit will teach them the necessary lessons to become equipped as church leaders.

On the church aboard *MOL Integrity*, for example, the leadership was strong. One second officer watched and learned in silence from these leaders until his contract ended. He did not have any official training, but he was so encouraged by what

God did on *MOL Integrity* that he immediately started a church on his next ship. His experience of church convinced him of the necessity of church on board. He saw the love among the crew and the changes in people. He saw, for example, how God changed a seafarer who always drank too much alcohol and had relationships with many women. When I met with this second officer I saw not only how he had grown in his faith, but also his deep desire to see people being saved and adding to their church on the ship. He shared some of the spiritual attacks he feels, but he was determined to press on and trusted that God would guide him as to how he should lead the church. God, in his time and wisdom, sent two other dedicated Christians who supported him in running this new church on the *MOL Solution.*

Port missionaries play a vital role in establishing churches on board. Missionaries and pastors need to train these leaders carefully through Bible studies, personal conversations and prayer so that they will get sufficient spiritual food. Many times seafarers just need that extra bit of encouragement and prayer before they start a church. Often they need more good solid teaching from the word of God. We could see many more churches formed, if only more missionaries shared this vision.

14

Difficulties in Planting Churches and Keeping them Alive

Missionary and church-planting work is not easy. Some spend many years preparing the ground before they are finally able, by God's grace, to start a church. A friend of mine who wanted to start a church in Hamburg, Germany needed ten years instead of the five years he had anticipated to establish a church. If planting churches is difficult on shore, how much more so on ships.

Even when churches are finally established on ships, though, they may only exist for a period of a year before the seafarers in charge go home for vacation. But this doesn't have to be the case. On one ship in particular, I witnessed God sending a constant stream of Christian crew members so that the church continued. It is amazing to see how God works as we recognize that the work of building the church is in his hands. On some ships when, from a human perspective, the best and most mature Christians left for vacation God in his wisdom sent other, perhaps less likely, people who continued the church.

But there are sometimes very practical reasons why a church cannot be established on a ship. The work schedules of the officers and crew, for example, often contradict each other. If one group works from 4:00 to 8:00[24] both morning and evening, and the other group works from 8:00 to 12:00 both morning and evening, it will be almost impossible to get together for church. The only possible time to meet in this case would be between 12

---

[24] On cargo and passenger ships seafarers usually work different watches – 4:00 to 8:00 a.m./4:00 to 8:00 p.m., 8:00 p.m. to 12 midnight/ 8:00 a.m. to 12 noon, 12 noon to 4:00 p.m./12 midnight to 4:00 a.m.

noon and 4:00 p.m. But even this time often will not work out
because the seafarers that work from 4:00 to 8:00 might still be
sleeping or might even have to work overtime. When a situation
like this occurs and seafarers cannot meet with other Christians
on board they can easily become frustrated and discouraged. I
have seen this happen on many different cargo and passenger
ships. They need encouragement, prayer and teaching from the
word of God.

Fear of superiors is another common reason why churches
are not started on board. On the passenger ship *Black Watch* I met
with several Christian seafarers and suggested that they start a
church on board. They all agreed that it would be good to do
so, but for reasons I could not quite understand they feared the
captain. When I offered to talk with the captain myself, they were
eager for me to do so. When I asked the captain for permission
for the seafarers to meet for Bible study, he agreed without any
hesitation. The crew was overjoyed with the news, and we met
that very evening. Eleven people attended – some from the
Philippines and some from Indonesia. One Indonesian Muslim
said, 'Actually I am not allowed to attend these meetings, but I
like to hear more.' When I left the ship after our first meeting they
were all in agreement that they would meet again. When I met
them several weeks later in another port, however, I found out
that the meeting had stopped. Although they had the desire to
meet with each other and learn from the word of God, there was
no Christian among them who was mature enough in the faith
and who had the vision to start and lead such a ship church. This
was a good lesson for me, as I realized that as a port chaplain I
needed to get more involved in identifying and equipping the
one that the Lord wants to be the 'spiritual leader' or elder. This
individual has to have a vision for the church on that particular
ship.

Again, God works mightily in this aspect of church planting
too, and I have witnessed this on several ships in particular. Once
I have identified this potential leader I meet with him regularly
and teach him more about discipleship and God's desire for a
church on board ship. On a huge coal ship called the *Rhine Ore*, I
met with Antonio Areglo, a third engineer from the Philippines.
He had a strong desire for fellowship and also wanted his crew

to know more about Jesus. That evening I visited Antonio again and we invited four other people who had been reading the Bible to meet with us. One of them was a believer as well. We talked together about the possibility of starting a ship church on board and read several passages from the book of Acts. They were all enthusiastic about the idea of having church on board. So, finally, after Bible study and prayer I appointed Antonio as their 'leader' – and then I had to leave. Before I left I gave them practical and theological advice on how to keep a church running on the ship. When I arrived home that night I learned that my wife had been praying fervently through the evening that God would send me to the right people at the right time. Antonio had also been praying that God would send people to the ship. It was a privilege to be there to be part of the answer to those prayers. Although the group had seemed to be very excited to come together regularly for prayer, fellowship and teaching of God's word, I never heard from the ship again. Although this is usually a sign that nothing was started, I might be wrong. It could also be that they sent letters which were lost, which happens not infrequently with letters sent from ships. One Nigerian seafarer I know wrote six letters to me, not one of which ever reached me. Establishing phone contact can also be difficult. So this is one ship and group of brothers I need to leave completely in God's hands, trusting and praying that God goes with them and continues to encourage them.

Christian seafarers wishing to start a church can experience problems with their superiors. Some really fear someone in a position of authority on the ship, such as the captain or the chief engineer. On one Nigerian ship, a dedicated Christian wanted to start a church, but when his superiors heard about it they started to treat him badly. They made him work more hours than necessary and he felt persecuted for the name of Christ. Christians working on ships under superiors who follow other religions can find it particularly difficult to start a church. It is not impossible, as we have seen from the example of the church on the *Al Mutanabbi*, but it requires lots of courage and faith to take that first step and persevere. Some Christian seafarers need to make more money, to send home for example, and so want promotions to earn better salaries. They might fear not getting their promotion because they are preaching Christ on the ship. Seafarers sometimes even fear losing their jobs because of their Christian activity. This is a real problem, since they seldom are able to find jobs at home.

Sometimes, too, a church is established and seafarers grow and enjoy the fellowship and then the captain hears about the church and, for whatever reason, orders them to stop. This happened on a reefer ship with which I was in contact. Several crew members met regularly for Bible study and prayer and then, all of a sudden, the captain (who professed to be a Christian) did not allow them to meet anymore. This created tension between the people who met in church and the captain. A church on a ship is always in some way subject to the human authority of the captain. I later learned that the captain, who belonged to a particular Christian group in the Philippines, did not agree with the theology of the church on his ship.

As we saw on the *QE2*, where different denominational backgrounds were causing problems, theological differences can stunt the growth of God's church on the oceans. On another ship I saw the church attendance gradually decrease because the strict legalism of the 'pastor' of this church created a stiff, unloving atmosphere. He shouted at people and made different laws that Christians were required to follow. When that man went home for vacation the church immediately began to grow in numbers again, and God's word went forth.

Another ever-present problem, for seafarers as for the rest of us, is sin. Over the last 16 years I have seen even the strongest and most mature Christians stop sharing their faith when they have fallen into a lifestyle or particular pattern of sin. Christians from some cultures feel such shame that they cannot find the strength to confess their sin and go on with Jesus. One seafarer was so happy to meet me and asked me to come to his cabin for prayer. He joyfully praised God and enjoyed the fellowship, yet the next day he did not want to see me because he had been with a prostitute. Seafarers live in such close quarters that if one does fall into such sin many others are watching him carefully and often criticise that person – even though they are probably committing the same sin themselves. Port chaplains and others involved in ministry to seafarers need to make sure, therefore, that they do everything possible to strengthen Christian seafarers in their faith and motivate them to continue with church on the ship, even when they have fallen into some kind of problem. I usually encourage people I meet with to confess everything directly and immediately to Christ. Then I share with them the many Bible verses in which God promises that he will never leave us and that he always forgives, regardless of how bad or damaging the particular sin might have been.

At this point it is important to note that even in ship churches seafarers need to have what the Bible calls church discipline. Without church discipline, the behaviour of some people would damage the church and give the church a bad reputation. Church on ships is something holy that should not be defiled by sin.

One Filipino Christian lived on a huge passenger ship for some time without telling others that he was a Christian. When he did share his faith with others, God blessed his testimony and a church was established. Here is what he has to say:

> I read my Bible every morning but I did not show others that I was a Christian – until one morning I learned there were other Christians on board. I started to put Bible verses on a board and then met with the other Christians. We were visited a lot by David Hawkins from the Seamen's Center in Seward, Alaska. He was really instrumental in helping us get started with the church. He encouraged us a great deal; he gave us Christian materials; he invited us to church; and he helped us in many practical ways. Our church met from 8:30 p.m. to 12:00 midnight every Sunday night. We sang praise and worship songs and studied the Bible. We invited many others on the ship but they did not come. They asked what we were doing. We continued to pray for them and after a year they finally started to attend. Some were still asking what denominations we were from and so we explained that we are not meeting as a particular denomination but that we are Christians who believe in Christ our Saviour. Later more people attended and became Christians. We always made it very clear: this church is not promoting any particular sect or division of Christianity. Instead we are promoting Christ as our personal Saviour and Master. Today there are almost 30 seafarers attending the church on Sundays.

This port chaplain in Seward, David Hawkins, had no permit to visit one particular cruise ship due to strict security regulations. So the seafarers came to the Seamen's Center, where he taught them from the Bible. Because of this ministry in the Seamen's Center, people were encouraged to start a church on their ship. And so today on the *Carnival Spirit* there are two Spanish-speaking groups meeting regularly, at different times of the day, for worship and prayer. There is also another English-speaking group that has started to meet to study the Bible. All of these folks came to the Seamen's Center and took piles of materials back to the ship with them, as this was their last visit before heading south.

Seafarers need an extra measure of encouragement because they are far away from family and friends and church at home. Christian seafarers can feel particularly isolated, and peer pressure and fear of their mates take on a different dimension because they live and work with them day in and day out. What will everybody say, Christian seafarers wonder, when I start a church on board? Again and again seafarers have confessed to me that this is one of their major problems. And this fear is not always unfounded. A Filipino Christian who worked on a Greek ship once told me that he wanted to share his faith, but his mates were so cruel to him that they took his food away and even tried to attack him. It was difficult to encourage him to live his faith. Once Christians are able to overcome this fear of their mates, however, they generally feel greatly encouraged and motivated. I remember one Nigerian ship in particular on which there were two believers. They belonged to different tribes, and perhaps that was one reason they did not start a church together. I went through the Scriptures to explain how important it was for them to meet together on the ship, but they didn't seem to understand. It took a long time to convince them. But, when they finally did start to meet, they wrote a joy-filled letter from Russia telling me how God has blessed their ship and how they now meet regularly with seven other people to worship God.

On some ships there are churches that do not call themselves churches for fear of being labelled heretics. They might instead refer to their meetings as Bible sharing or Bible study. Sometimes they do not use the word 'church' because they feel they need a pastor in order to call it a church. It often takes a considerable investment of time sharing and teaching from the Bible to convince seafarers of the need of a church on board. Once they have seen the need and understand that this is what the Bible says, they are more willing to start.

As you read of the various difficulties confronting churches on board ships, you may be asking what you can do to support them. First of all, this ministry among seafarers is not very well known. Therefore, it is of the utmost importance that Christians all over the world pray for more missionaries who can start churches on ships and encourage and support them on shore. But, in addition to prayer, there are several ways Christians can be involved in supporting the existing missionaries. I have taken several Christians along with me on ships to see ship churches, and they were always encouraged to see what God is doing among these dear seafarers. So if you live in a port you could find out whether or not there is a ministry there to seafarers. If so, you could ask the port missionary how you could help the mission and the seafarers. If there is no mission yet, you could enlist the help of your local church to spread the good news of Christ among seafarers. If you are in touch with seafarers you could also write to them and thus be a great encouragement to them.

15

Opportunities and Challenges

The churches on the oceans as a tool to reach the least reached

In both the Old and the New Testaments we read that it is God's desire that people in even the furthest corners of the world should worship God. In Isaiah 66:19 God challenges Israel to take his message to the islands who have not heard of him: 'I will set a sign among them and I will send some of those who survive to the nations – to Tarshish, to the Libyans, and Lydians, to Tubal and Greece, and to the distant islands that have not heard of my fame or seen my glory.' In Psalm 105:1 we read the following: 'Give thanks to the Lord, call on his name, make known among the nations what he has done.' And Psalm 2:8 says: 'Ask of me and I will make the nations your inheritance.' In the New Testament we see the so-called mission commands, for instance Matthew 28:29: 'therefore go and make disciples of all nations, baptizing them in the name of the Father, and of the Son and of the Holy Spirit.' Acts 1:8 makes it clear that God always has the whole world in mind: 'But you will receive power when the Holy Spirit will come on you and you will be my witnesses in Jerusalem, and in all Judea, and Samaria and to the ends of the earth.'

9. A visit to the church on board the *Golden Princess*

The church and mission agencies do not question that it is God's desire to reach the least reached with the gospel. In fact, they encourage Christians in their desire to reach these remote people. Yet it is not easy to reach them. Ships, however, can carry the gospel in a very natural way, without tremendous costs in terms of time or travel, to places we would seldom go. Time after time seafarers have asked me for tracts and Christian materials so that they can evangelize in the countries their ship will visit. As long as ships and planes are moving, the gospel has no limits.

If, for instance, a church on a ship takes Jesus' command to evangelize seriously, there are many ways in which this ship church will be able to reach the unreached with the gospel. They might go to places like China, with its millions of people. They might bring written materials such as tracts and Bibles to this spiritually needy country, and they could also visit and encourage Christians and churches there. Seamen have told me many times that they are absolutely free to travel in China once their ship is berthed. They could thus take the gospel to many people who are in need. The same is possible in other countries as well. Even in places where seamen do not have the freedom to travel in the country itself, they can talk to the local people who come on board for business and share Christ with them. Many seamen have told us about how they have done just that and were able to pass on literature.

Port chaplains, in fact, have a two-fold purpose. First of all, they are to bring the gospel of salvation to seafarers and to help plant churches on ships wherever it is possible. But secondly, and perhaps just as importantly, they are to train seafarers to become missionaries in countries to which their ships are sailing. Seafarers can bring the gospel to other countries much more effectively, as they often speak the language and know the culture. They are often much more welcome in these countries than 'westerners', since they know how to behave and operate in a foreign culture. Through these seafarers, who work in their jobs but also share Christ in foreign ports, the gospel is being brought to the farthest corners of the world. We can train seafarers to be missionaries in Shanghai, Dubai, Tokyo, Los Angeles or St Petersburg – depending on where their ship is going.

But, since all seafarers go home after eight or ten months on board, if we train them to live their faith at home the gospel will reach places of which we have never even dreamed. I have personally heard several testimonies of seafarers who came to know Christ on board ships and then went home and led their family members to Christ. A few of these even went on to plant churches in their home towns. Many of these seafarers, however, experienced a time of testing when they began to share their new-found faith at home. Some were mocked and even kicked out of their families because of their faith. One man from a Muslim country who came to know Christ while he was working on a ship wrote to my co-worker asking him not to write to him at home – because such correspondence would make his life as a Christian even more difficult. In some ways this sort of persecution is to be expected, for there are few better opportunities to reach the unreached in China, Russia, India, Egypt, the Philippines and other countries with the good news of Jesus Christ than through their own people – the seafarers.

God extends his grace in amazing ways to those who are called to suffer for his sake. We met seafarers from a Muslim country who took the gospel home and were fined and immediately put into prison. When we met them again on another ship a few years later, they were strong in their faith and eager for another opportunity to take the gospel home. Thus far we have been in touch with seafarers from about 150 different countries. Because these men love their families and friends and want them to know the love of Jesus Christ, we can be sure that the gospel of salvation has been brought to these 150 countries around the world. Missionaries would not be allowed to travel to many of these countries, but when we place the written word of God into the hands of Muslims, Hindus, Buddhists and others, then they will carry the gospel to almost every place in the world. God opens an infinite number of doors through seamen's ministry.

What can the church on shore do to help the church at sea?

The majority of churches worldwide have never heard about churches on the oceans. Another important task for the various seamen's missions, seafarers and missionaries, therefore, is to make these churches known to churches on shore. While Christians around the world are anxious to see churches planted among Muslims, Hindus and other religious groups, they know very little, if anything, about how this is happening on the oceans. Thousands of churches pray for other churches that are planted around the world, but they can only offer prayer support and practical help if they are well informed. Relationships between shore and ship churches can be mutually beneficial, bringing many blessings and much fruit.

Once a bigger or more established church begins to build a relationship with a younger or smaller church they are supporting, they adopt a certain responsibility before the Lord to do all they can to help this church grow and prosper. They provide practical resources as appropriate as well as encouragement; they rejoice with them in the Lord's work and evidence of fruit; and they even suffer with them through the hard times of trial. They strengthen the relationship by encouraging visits between the two churches. This kind of partnership between churches is a strong and biblical model.

What kind of partnership might a church on the oceans have with a church on shore? Would a church on shore take them on as their partner? There would need to be some sort of link or bridge between the church on shore and the church on the sea to make the relationship work – and so the port missionary would probably function as this bridge. The port missionary, with information about both churches, could offer suggestions as to how the land-based church could help and motivate the ship church, and vice versa. He could communicate prayer items and practical information to both churches and arrange for members of each church to write to one another. Meeting the seafarers and hearing their testimonies would encourage the church on shore to stand behind this ministry on the ship. This would only be possible, of course, if the seafarers were in port when the church on shore was meeting. Such a partnership would probably only work for churches that are located in port cities.

The church on shore that did establish such a partnership, however, would find itself in a vital and strategic position to encourage a ship church to grow strong in faith and multiply to the glory of God. There are a number of ways a church could be involved. First of all, they could have a designated team to maintain regular contact with the port missionary and keep the ship's prayer items alive. This team could also inform those in a position to help about practical needs, like clothes and woolly hats, and have them ready when the ship comes into port.

As a port missionary, I am the bridge between the ship churches and our local church and have seen this in action. When I share the needs and vision with my home church in Hamburg and challenge the church to act, they do so. But I have also noticed that if I do not continue to share the vision of a ship's church, the vision quickly grows cold. So it is crucial for the missionary to keep the vision alive and challenge both churches to support each other.

One powerful way of strengthening the relationship between the two churches is to have a church member from ashore sail with the ship. Today many ships have spare cabins and some, in fact, even have special tourist cabins. So the church member could sail two, three or more weeks with the ship and thus get to know the seafarers and their situation on board. He would begin to understand the difficulties and joys of a seafarer and would most probably pray more intensively for them. He would learn how a ship church can function and he would be able to encourage, teach and, if necessary, admonish the believers on board. He could then report back to his own church in a way that would bridge the gaps in knowledge and understanding. This would be a tremendous encouragement for both churches. If these visits continued and were quite regular, perhaps once a year, I see no reason why we should not see strong, living churches sailing the oceans. Today we see similar things happening with churches who support other churches around the world. They go on short-term mission trips and 'adopt a people group'. Why should the churches on shore not adopt another people group – the seafarers?

In the early 1980s, a church in Hamburg established a wonderful relationship with a church on a Nigerian ship. The sailors came into port every two to three months, and the church usually invited the seafarers for Bible studies on shore. People from the shore church invited individual seafarers to come to their homes to enjoy fellowship. Some church members also helped seafarers with practical needs, such as clothes and mailing their letters. When the seafarers were at sea, and even when they went home on vacation, church members wrote them letters of encouragement. Even today, I meet Nigerians who still ask me about that particular church in Hamburg and remember certain church members by name. One of the beautiful moments we enjoyed with this lovely Nigerian ship church was when the ship church invited the shore church for a meal on the ship. We ate together and laughed together, and the officers showed us around their ship. We enjoyed Christian fellowship through Bible studies, personal testimonies and a lot of singing and prayer.

Another of these relationships blossomed between a church in Cape Town and a ship church. Here is what Kurt and Thea Schönhoff, missionaries among seafarers, experienced when the passenger ship *Universal Explorer* came to Cape Town on different occasions.

> *February 2002:* We arranged to have daily meetings on board and Alan, a Filipino who was in charge of the ship church, suggested that it would be best to meet at 3:00 p.m. every afternoon. They also organized sport activities every afternoon and the Christians were encouraged by these meetings.

November 2002: For the first time the ship was here on a Sunday, so we discussed the possibility of bringing a group from a local church on board. Alan said that we must bring the choir from the church. Never have the church members turned into a choir so fast, although with all the musical talent we have that was really not a problem. The staff captain gave the permission and we had to fax through the names of 20 people 24 hours before the event which, in this case, was on a Sunday evening. We visited and had fellowship with the Christians every day. The Sunday evening went off very well and one seaman accepted the Lord afterwards while we were having some snacks and there was time to talk. He is still going on for the Lord according to Alan. Besides singing, one of our local church members gave a message.

February 2003: This time the ship was not here on a Sunday. However, yet again we were able to come aboard and lead a meeting and about 50 seafarers attended. Again we visited the ship every day.

Alan, the ship church leader, wrote the following to Kurt and Thea: 'The church on board *Universal Explorer* was truly blessed. Thank you for the wonderful time we had in Cape Town; these were unforgettable moments in our life. The crew were all so happy. We will help Joel to make his faith stronger with my brothers here. We will work together to get more souls involved in God's work.'

Kurt and Thea continue: 'Joel was saved that night, and we have heard since that he is growing in the Lord. This was the response after 20 members of our church were allowed on board to sing and preach one evening. Some time later Alan sent another email: "We are heading to your place and we can't wait to see you again, our dwelling and refuelling place...thanks to God for giving us some wonderful people and place to dwell on." We were able to take another team on board and once again the ship church and the local church team was blessed. On the last evening we offered to take 18 seafarers on a tour by night of Cape Town. Twenty-eight arrived and we got them all in but prayed all the way.'

* * *

One large Filipino church in Manila considers one of their members, Carlos F., as 'their' missionary that they sent out to reach seafarers for Christ. Carlos had already planted a church in the Philippines and, once becoming a seafarer, started right away to plant a church on the German container vessel he is sailing on. I met Carlos recently, and he told me that his home church prays regularly for the needs of the ship church that was planted. They not only pray for the ship church, but they also feel responsible to teach Carlos F. more from the word of God through audio tapes and through Christian books from the Navigators. Thus Carlos feels well equipped and encouraged to continue his spiritual work on board ship. Carlos' wife reports regularly to the home church in Manila about how the ship church is progressing. Carlos also receives encouragement and prayer and practical support for his church work on the ship from various port missionaries with whom he meets.

These are just a few examples of how bringing the resources of the people of God together can result in tremendous advancements for the gospel around the world.

A challenging idea

There are many people throughout the world who have made the effort to study foreign languages, foreign cultures and even different jobs. They become missionaries by going to work in countries and cultures where otherwise they would not be allowed to go. Especially in the countries of the so-called 10/40 window, people cannot officially enter as missionaries but can work as biologists, scientists, physicians or in other jobs. God has used hundreds and hundreds of dedicated Christians to bring the gospel to these countries in this way. Since 11 September 2001, many more countries have tightened security and visa regulations, and some would rather close their borders than open them for missionaries. In the future, therefore, the only way to share Christ in many countries might be through an official job – and even that might become difficult. As even radio and television and other methods of transmitting the good news become more and more difficult, Christians will need to think more creatively about other ways to reach the unreached.

Here is one challenging idea. Why should Bible colleges, universities and churches not call for people who are willing to sacrifice their lives to serve God on ships? Why should a man (or couple, if possible) not work as an ordinary seaman, officer or engineer with the goal of starting churches on ships? With the possible exception of Carlos F., from the Philippines, in all my years as a port chaplain I never met anybody who chose to become a seaman for the sake of sharing Christ, of being a missionary for other seamen and bringing the gospel to the least reached. I have never met anyone who became a seaman in order to plant churches. People who choose to be seafarers generally do so for financial reasons, not for missionary purposes. They want to support their families and give their children a better education. There is nothing wrong with that. Yet countless Christians have studied and pursued many different jobs and professions for the sole purpose of bringing the gospel to a particular people, tribe or country. Why should people who are passionate about reaching a particular country or even a continent with the gospel not become seafarers?

The people a seafarer missionary would meet on a ship are completely free to listen and to accept the gospel. Seafarers are subject to very little, if any, cultural, religious or political pressure. No one polices them as long as they serve on the ship for the period of their contract. The advantages are clear. A missionary who works as a seaman has plenty of time to share Christ for the duration of his contract. He can build friendships with seamen from different cultures and countries and eventually even build ship churches while he is sailing with them. A seafarer missionary would share his home with others, seeing the people whom he wants to reach for Christ every day and having countless opportunities to live out and share his faith. He would eat and work with them. He would have, in the best sense, a 'captive audience' for the gospel. As we have seen again and again, seafarers need the gospel, and they need the fellowship of a church in their home on the seas. So maybe we need to go the extra mile and choose a job we would not have normally chosen.

Seafarer missionaries would receive salaries and would therefore be able to support themselves and would not depend on churches, mission societies or individuals for their financial needs. They might not even need a mission agency. But they would need churches that support their vision and a church, or at least a mission group, that would pray regularly for them.

10. *Saga Rose* – the captain of this ship had a desire to see the ship's church grow

While the advantages and opportunities are clear, so are the sacrifices that would be required. It is not, of course, an easy job. Working on board ship means hard work and often many extra hours. It would also require adapting to different cultures and living with people from all nationalities. It would mean eating the same food as the rest of the crew and officers, it would mean giving up a certain amount of freedom and privacy. It would also mean leaving friends and family at home and living apart for maybe six, eight or even twelve months.

It would be ideal if two or three Christians could work together on one ship. They could encourage and help each other even in times of disappointment. Because of the inherent difficulties and challenges, jobs at sea are generally available for those who are looking at this career to gain access to ships for the purpose of church planting among the unreached. Unemployment and general economic factors also affect jobs at sea as well as on shore.

Many Christians worldwide have served on Christian ships through Operation Mobilisation or Mercy Ships. These people have experience as seamen and as part-time 'evangelists'. They would find it even easier to take that step of faith to be missionaries on cargo or passenger ships. In the future, these big mission agencies might train their people for missionary work on other ships as well as on their own ships. In this way they could make a tremendous contribution towards reaching the least reached. Churches could be planted on cargo and passenger ships alike. Just imagine what could result if Bible colleges offered courses in world mission as tent makers on ships? After finishing their jobs on deck or in the engine room, these missionaries could pastor a church on the very same ship. This is, of course, a challenge more likely to be taken up by people who are not married. A man who is married and has children needs to take care of his family, and it is rather unlikely that he would want to be away from them for such a long time. But there are possibilities for couples to work, for instance, on cruise ships. I look forward to the day when missionary societies recruit personnel for such work on board ships to reach the forgotten people of the world.

If a man takes up the challenge to be a missionary on a ship, he will also learn a lot which he might use in his home church. He will certainly learn a tremendous amount of flexibility. He will learn to love and esteem other cultures and other people who have totally different ways of life. Once he has experienced an international ship church, he will know how to integrate foreigners in a church on shore as well. He will learn how to approach and live with people from all over the world. The shore church would benefit from the wealth of experience he will have gained while being a missionary to seafarers from different countries. He would be able to connect his home church to ship churches, nurturing those important relationships between churches we explored above.

Is taking up the call to be a seafarer really too challenging? Is it too big a sacrifice to make for our Saviour, who gave up everything for us?

16

A New Vision for Both Seafarers and Missionaries

There are those who believe that you cannot teach an old dog new tricks. Sadly, I have met some missionaries who do not want to work with other missionaries, who resist trying new ideas, and who have even declared that they cannot change. Several years ago I met one particular missionary and invited him to work together with a network of missionaries to establish better follow-up with seafarers. He replied, 'I've worked on my own for the last twenty-five years and I don't intend to change that now.' Obviously missionaries need to be more flexible and willing to learn from the Lord and from other mature Christians if this vision of churches on ships is to become reality.

Many missionaries have dedicated their lives to bringing the gospel of salvation to as many seafarers as possible and have made many sacrifices to do so. They have used their gifts and talents to present the gospel in many different ways and God has blessed their efforts by bringing many to Christ. Yet I believe that the strategic focus for work among seafarers in the twenty-first century is on building his church on ships. This people group has been neglected in many ways, and I cannot imagine what it must be like to spend 30 years and more at sea without having the chance to attend church. God cannot be satisfied with the fact that thousands and thousands live on the oceans without having a church.

But the question is this: Who will share this vision of building churches with missionaries and seafarers? What we have done in the past among seafarers was good, and God has blessed this work, but now we need to go new ways. You who have read this book are in a unique position to understand how important churches on board are for seafarers. Even seafarers who have been living out their Christian lives on board in different ways need to adopt a new way of thinking. The challenge is to see the possibilities of God's way, of having a church on board. In Acts 20:28 we read an exhortation from God that applies to missionaries among seafarers. 'Keep watch over yourselves and all the flock of which the Holy Spirit has made you overseers. Be shepherds of the church of God, which he bought with his own blood.' This is actually a command of God. The apostle Paul was talking here to the elders of the Ephesian church, reminding them that they were to oversee and shepherd the church.

In the same way, God has challenged us to be shepherds for the church at sea. Since at the very beginning of a church there are no elders, we fulfil that role as overseers of the church at sea. If we are shepherds of the church at sea, then we must surely nurture the church and give them the necessary food so that they can grow as a church and as individuals. The word 'shepherd' implies that we should take care of the sheep, the Christians under our care, in such a way that they grow into a healthy relationship with God and with one another. God speaks about shepherding his church, and not just a Bible study or fellowship group. Jesus purchased these ship churches with his own blood. God has made port chaplains overseers over this flock, the living church on the oceans. This is a strong challenge. God wants to be glorified by seafarers in his church.

For some seafarers the prospect of a church on board is exciting; some long for it and have caught the vision already. But for many others it is a totally new concept. They need to understand why it is important to start a church on board, and then they need to learn how to start a church. This will take time, but the Holy Spirit is the greatest teacher. God knows that missionaries do not have sufficient time with seafarers due to their hectic schedules and limited time in ports.

I witnessed the truth and power of God's provision of the Holy Spirit to teach with Saroh Diaz on the *MOL Integrity*. Saroh did not know what salvation meant. After he was saved, the Holy Spirit started to teach him through various Bible correspondence courses that he studied that it is important not only to share the faith but also to have a place of worship on the ship and to start God's church. I met Saroh every two months and tried to encourage him to do so, but God was the one who encouraged and taught him. If I had told people that somebody who had been a Christian for just nine months should start a church, nobody would have agreed with me. They would have said, 'This isn't going to work; he's too young and immature.' They would have said that he needed to grow in faith or even to attend Bible college before he could act as a 'pastor' or leader of the ship congregation. If we had waited, then it is unlikely there would be a church on that ship today. God surely is doing the extraordinary in people in extraordinary situations.

The chief cook on the *Al Mutanabbi* who started a church after being a Christian for four years is another such example of God's amazing grace. I did not tell him to start the church. I was even more surprised to see that he was following God's call to start a training class for those who wanted more spiritual food. He had the desire to make disciples and to see 2 Timothy 2:2 put into practice. 'And the things you have heard me say in the presence of many witnesses entrust to reliable men who will also be qualified to teach others.' So he faithfully gathers Christians for training in evangelism and in prayer with the goal of equipping these believers so that, when they are on different ships, they will be able to start new churches.

11. *Al Mutanabbi* – God planted a church on this ship through one faithful Filipino Christian

Although God did teach these two men in extraordinary ways, we still have a responsibility to use our time and resources and opportunities to teach such potential leaders as we are able. It would be too easy to simply say that God will do his work. God called us to start teaching seafarers in order to establish churches on board ships. We have a responsibility which we want to carry out to make disciples of all nations and to encourage and equip believers to start ship churches wherever they are. If we are faithful in training seafarers to start churches on board, these seafarers will carry the gospel far and wide – across the oceans and to faraway lands as well.

Imagine what could happen if the ship church was a training field for church planters worldwide. There are several maritime training academies in the Philippines led by born-again Christians. They teach seafarers the word of God. How wonderful it would be if they would also train them to start churches on the ships on which they will sail. In the same way, local churches could train their members who are seafarers, or who might be called to be seafarer missionaries, to be church planters on ships. If churches would assume this responsibility, they would make a huge contribution to world evangelization. Actually the foundation of this vision is a triangle: the church at home, the seafarer and the port chaplain. These three should work together in different ways to see God's church established around the world. To God be the glory!

Appendix: Defining 'Church'

The following outline is reproduced with kind permission of Rob Flinders, port chaplain of SCFS in Sydney, Australia.

What is 'church'?

What does the word 'church' mean? Some people talk about the 'Catholic' church or the 'Protestant' church, or different parts of the Protestant church, like the 'Baptist' or the 'Presbyterian' or the 'Methodist' churches. Some people think that 'church' is the building in which believers meet.

The Bible never uses the word 'church' in these ways.

'Church' is a group of believers

In the Bible the word 'church' is always used to describe people – people who believe what God says about his only Son Jesus Christ and who have repented of their sins and put their faith in Jesus Christ as their Saviour and Lord.

In the Bible these people are sometimes called 'believers' (Acts 1:15; 4:32; 5:12). Sometimes they are called 'brothers or sisters' (Colossians 1:2; 1 Thessalonians 1:4; 5:25; James 1:2). Sometimes they are called 'Christians' (Acts 11:26; 26:28; 1 Peter 4:16). Sometimes they are called 'disciples' (Matthew 28:19–20; John 8:31; Acts 11:26) and sometimes they are called 'saints' (Romans 1:7; 2 Corinthians 1:1; Ephesians 1:1; Philippians 1:1).

These different words all have the same meaning. All of them are names for people who have repented and put their faith in the Lord Jesus Christ.

'Church' is the 'family of God'

The Bible says that when a person repents and puts his faith in the Lord Jesus Christ as his Saviour and Lord, he is made alive again spiritually (Ephesians 2:1–10). The Bible also describes this as being born again spiritually (1 Peter 1:23). When a person is made alive again his name is written in the Lamb's Book of Life in heaven (Revelation 21:27).

The Bible says that when a person is made alive again he becomes a child of God. Now God is his heavenly Father (Romans 8:16). Other believers are now his brothers and sisters in Christ.

The church is like a huge family, made up of all true believers in the Lord Jesus Christ from all over the world, regardless of their nationality, colour, race or language, including those who have already died. This is sometimes called 'the invisible church'.

Here on earth it is impossible for this church to ever meet in one place and at one time, but one day in the future it will meet – in heaven. On that day it will be 'a great multitude that no-one could count, from every nation, tribe, people and language' (Revelation 7:9).

Some other descriptions of 'church'

In Ephesians 2:19-22 believers are described as 'members of God's household, built on the foundation of the apostles and the prophets, with Christ Jesus himself as the chief cornerstone. In him the whole building is joined together and rises to become a holy temple in the Lord. And in him you too are being built together to become a dwelling in which God lives by his Spirit.'

Sometimes the Bible describes the church as the 'body of Christ' and Jesus Christ as 'the head of the body, the church' (Colossians 1:18,24).

The Bible says that the Lord Jesus Christ is the only head of the church (Ephesians 1:22-23).

Local churches

In the Bible the word 'church' is used in two ways:

a) As we have seen, the word 'church' is used to describe all believers throughout history, whether still alive or dead. This is the invisible church, the church that is described as 'God's household' and the 'body of Christ.'

b) The word 'church' is also used to describe all the believers in a certain place at a certain time. It is possible for believers who live near to one another to meet together in one place at one time. This is what we call a 'local church'.

The New Testament contains several letters that were written to different local churches – to groups of believers who were meeting together.

The apostle Paul wrote letters to the 'church of God in Corinth' (1 Corinthians 1:2). He also wrote a letter to the 'churches in Galatia' (Galatians 1:2).

Paul also wrote a letter to the church at Ephesus (the book of Ephesians), one to the church at Philippi (the book of Philippians), one to the church at Colossae (the book of Colossians) and two letters to the church at Thessalonica (the books of 1 and 2 Thessalonians).

House churches

The New Testament tells us that sometimes believers met together in people's houses. When they met together in this way these believers were meeting as a church.

In his letter to the Romans, Paul talks about Priscilla and Aquila and 'the church in their house' (Romans 16:5 and 1 Corinthians 16:19).

In his letter to the Colossians Paul talks about Nympha and 'the church in her house' (Colossians 4:15).

In his letter to Philemon Paul talks about 'the church in your house' (Philemon 1:2).

Again we see from this that church is a group of believers, not a building.

A group of believers can meet anywhere that is convenient. They can come together inside a public building, or outside in a public place, or they can come together in a private home. A group of believers can meet anywhere that is convenient for them. When they meet together as a group of believers they are a church.

When seafarers who are believers get together in a mess room, or a recreation room or in a cabin to worship God, to read and study the Bible and to pray, they are a church.

Even if there are only two or three believers meeting together, they are still a church. Jesus said, 'for where two or three come together in my name, there am I with them' (Matthew 18:20).

One body – many parts

We know that our physical bodies have many different parts and that each part has special work to do. Although there are many different parts, all of them belong to the one body.

The Bible says that the church is the body of Christ, that each believer is a part of that body and that each believer belongs to all the other believers (Romans 12:5 and 1 Corinthians 12:12-31).

The Bible also says that the Spirit of God has given each believer a spiritual gift – a special ability or talent. The Bible says he must use his gift to help other believers in the church (1 Peter 4:10).

Some believers have been given the gift of teaching. Some have been given the gift of evangelism. Some believers have the gift of helping and encouraging other people; other believers have the gift of administration and so on (Romans 12:3-8; 1 Corinthians 12:1-31).

Each believer is a very important and essential part of the church. He has important work to do. When all the believers in a church are doing their work well and are helping each other, then that church will be strong and healthy.

What should believers do when they meet together?

The Bible tells us that when the first believers met together several things happened. Acts 2:41-47; 4:32-35 tell us that –

- They worshipped God together
- They learned about the teaching of the apostles
- They prayed together
- They helped and encouraged each other
- They shared food together
- They shared their goods and possessions

The Bible also says that the believers 'spoke the word of God boldly' (Acts 4:23-31). This means that they talked to unbelievers about God's Son, Jesus Christ, and the importance of repentance and faith in him.

Today, when believers meet together as a church, they do these same things.

They worship God. They listen to God, when the Bible is read and preached. They talk to God, when they pray. They help and encourage each other to serve God and each other. Sometimes they share a meal together. This is called 'the Lord's Supper'.

Worshipping God

The Bible tells us to live holy lives by turning away from what we know is wrong and doing what we know is right instead. When we do this the Bible says our bodies are 'living sacrifices' and we are worshipping God (Romans 12:1-2).

The Bible says that believers also worship God when they come together as a church and sing psalms and hymns and spiritual songs with thankfulness in their hearts to God (Colossians 3:16; Ephesians 5:19-20).

Listening to God

The Bible says that God has spoken to us through his Son, the Lord Jesus Christ (Hebrews 1:1-3). Jesus shows us what God is like (John 1:18) and Jesus tells us everything God wants us to know.

Both the Old and New Testaments of the Bible tell us about Jesus Christ (John 5:39). When we read and study the Bible and learn about Jesus, God is speaking to us (John 17:14).

The Bible says, 'All Scripture is God-breathed and is useful for teaching, rebuking, correcting and training in righteousness, so that the man of God may be thoroughly equipped for every good work' (2 Timothy 3:16).

When we hear, read and study the Bible it is God speaking to us. This is a very important part of church.

Talking to God

Another important part of church is prayer. Prayer is a conversation between God and a believer (Philippians 4:6). The Bible says believers are God's children and that they can call God their 'heavenly Father' (Matthew 6:9; Romans 8:14-17).

When we talk to God we can praise him for who he is, for what he is like and for what he has done and is doing (Jude 24-25). We should also thank him (1 Thessalonians 5:17-18) and confess our sins to him (1 John 1:9). When we pray we can also tell God about our requests – for our own needs and the needs of others (Philippians 4:6).

The Bible can help us when we pray. It tells us how to praise God and how to thank him. It also shows us what we should ask God to do for us.

Encouraging one another

When believers meet together as a church they are able to encourage and help one another.

We have already seen that God wants each believer to use his spiritual gift to give help to other believers. He also needs to receive help from other believers. This can only happen if the believers meet together regularly. This is one reason why believers should meet together as a church.

Another reason believers should meet together is because it is not easy to be a believer. Over and over again the Bible reminds Christians that they are in a battle and that they are fighting against the world and the devil and his evil forces. We also have to fight against our old sinful nature (Ephesians 6:10-13; 2 Corinthians 10:3-4).

If we feel defeated or disheartened other believers can encourage us and remind us about the mercy and loving kindness of God and all the good that God has prepared for us.

That is why the Bible says, 'And let us consider how we may spur one another on towards love and good deeds. Let us not give up meeting together, as some are in the habit of doing, but let us encourage one another – and all the more as you see the Day [of Christ's return] approaching' (Hebrews 10:24-25).

Church is also an opportunity for believers to encourage and help one another to speak to non-believers about the Lord Jesus Christ (Acts 4:23-31).

Bible teaching about the church

For detailed information on what the Bible teaches about the church, please refer to one or more of the following Emmaus Bible study courses, which have been written to encourage seafarers who are believers and who meet together as a church on board their ship:

- Searching in the Bible [Lesson 7]: Church Fellowship
- The Christian Life [Lesson 6]: The Church
- Twelve Bottles of Spiritual Milk [Lesson 8]: The Church
- Lessons for Christian Living [Lesson 7]: Choosing a Church
- I'll Take the High Road [Lesson 12]: Enjoying the Fellowship
- Christ Loved the Church [All lessons]

These Emmaus resources can be found on the internet at:
http://www.emmausuk.org.uk
Tel: +44 151 327-1172 / Fax: +44 151 327-1592

You can also contact the author by email:
scfs.martin.otto@gmx.de
Or visit the author's website: www.seafarers-ministry.de

Also available from PIQUANT EDITIONS

Seafarers!
*A Strategic
Missionary Vision*

(now translated into 6
languages)
112 pp. paperback
ISBN-10: 0953575764
ISBN-13: 978 0953575763
www.piquanteditions.com

'Dear Mr Otto, I read your book *Seafarers! A Strategic Missionary Vision* and thank God for the calling which he has given to you and your fellow workers among the world's merchant seamen. Thank you also for writing the book and bringing about an awareness of the spiritual, emotional and physical needs of those "who go down to the sea in ships"'.

Captain Thomas Couchman, England

'I wasn't interested in your ministry until I read your book *Seafarers!* My husband didn't really tell me how hard life on a ship is, but when I read your book, I cried and prayed. I thank you for coming into his life. Your book has taught me to pray for him earnestly.'

Ann Villacarlos, wife of a seafarer from the Philippines